BEAUTIFUL POR

Realistic Adult Coloring Book

Women, Girls, Fairies and so much more

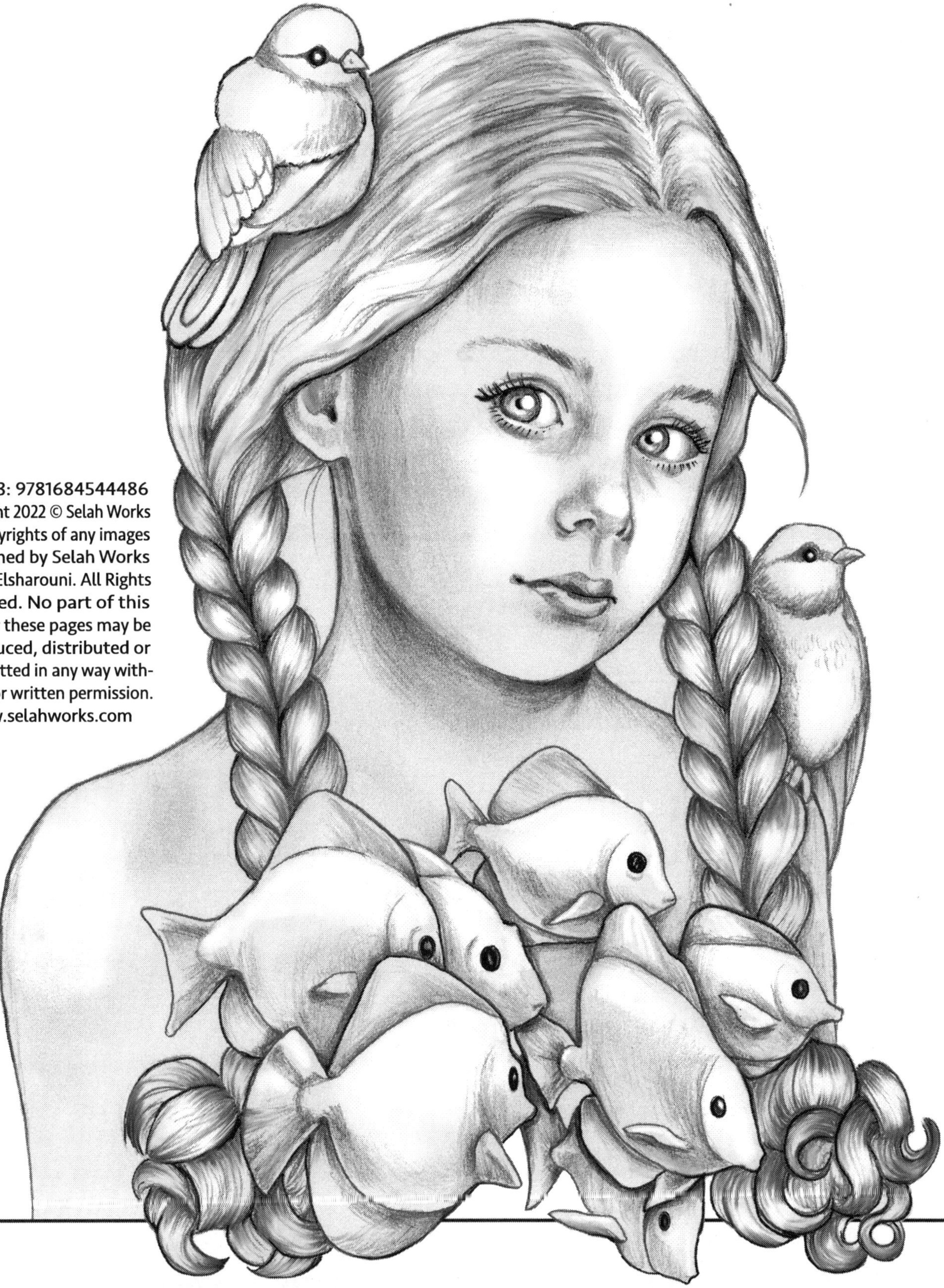

ISBN-13: 9781684544486

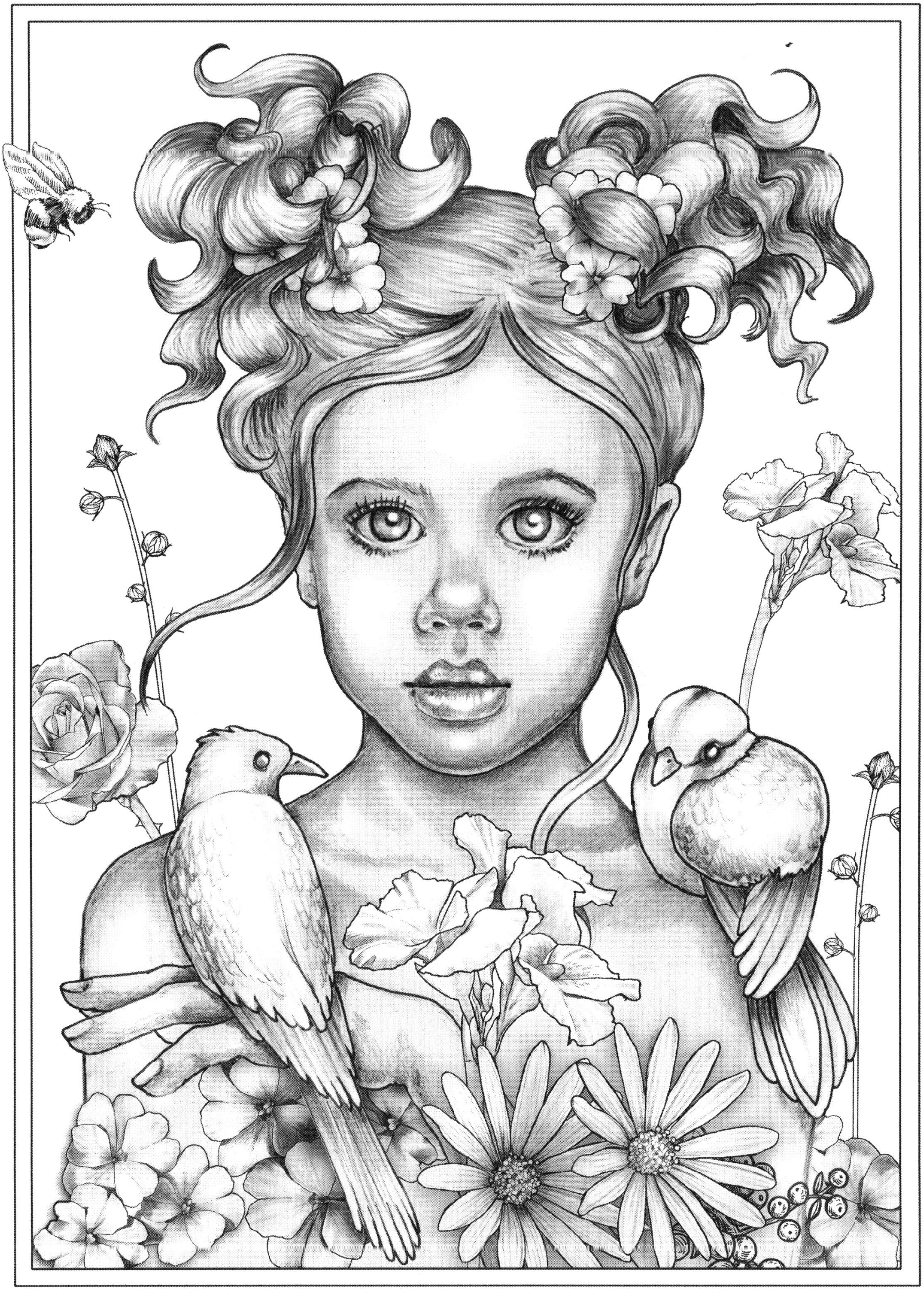

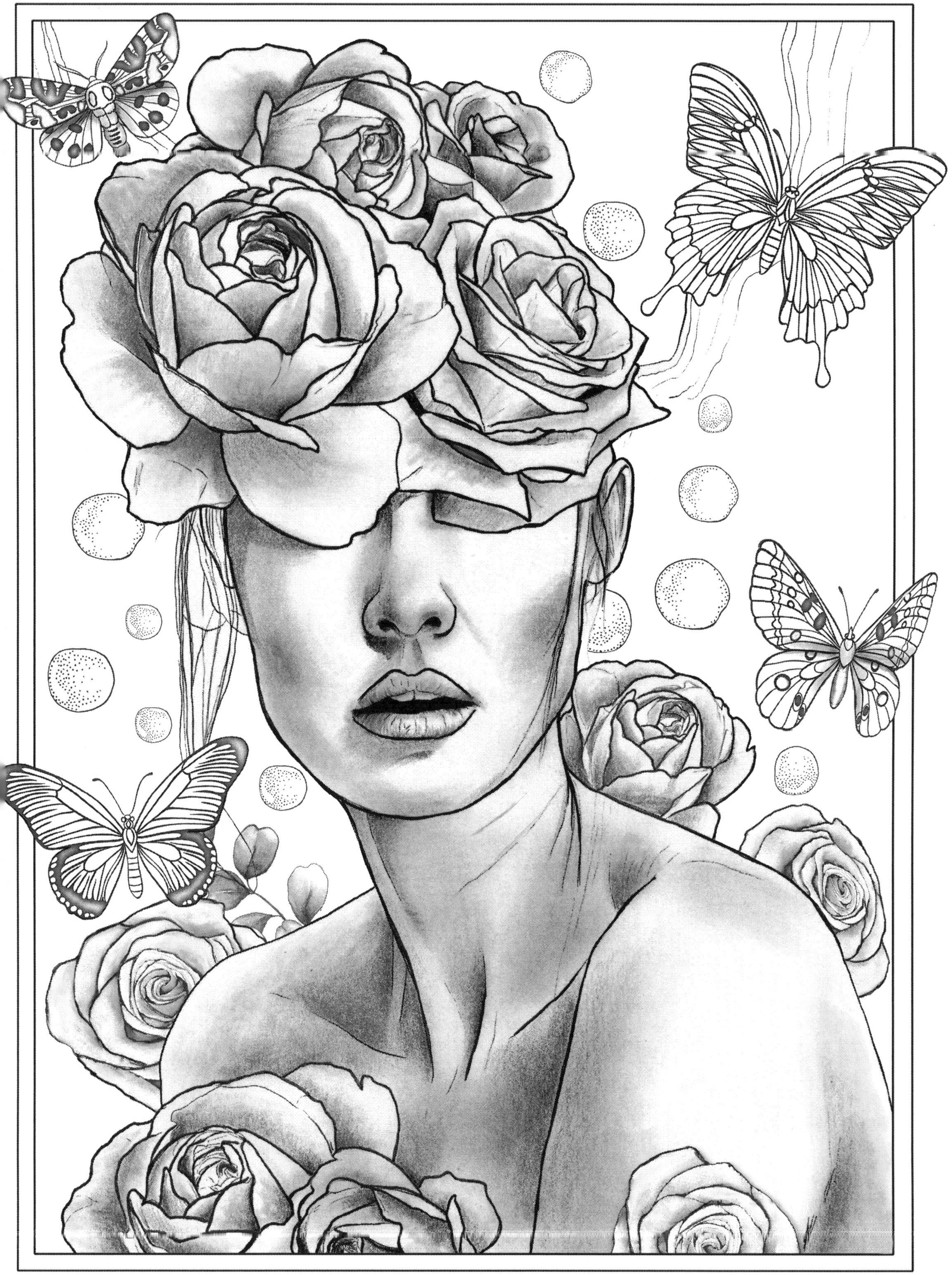

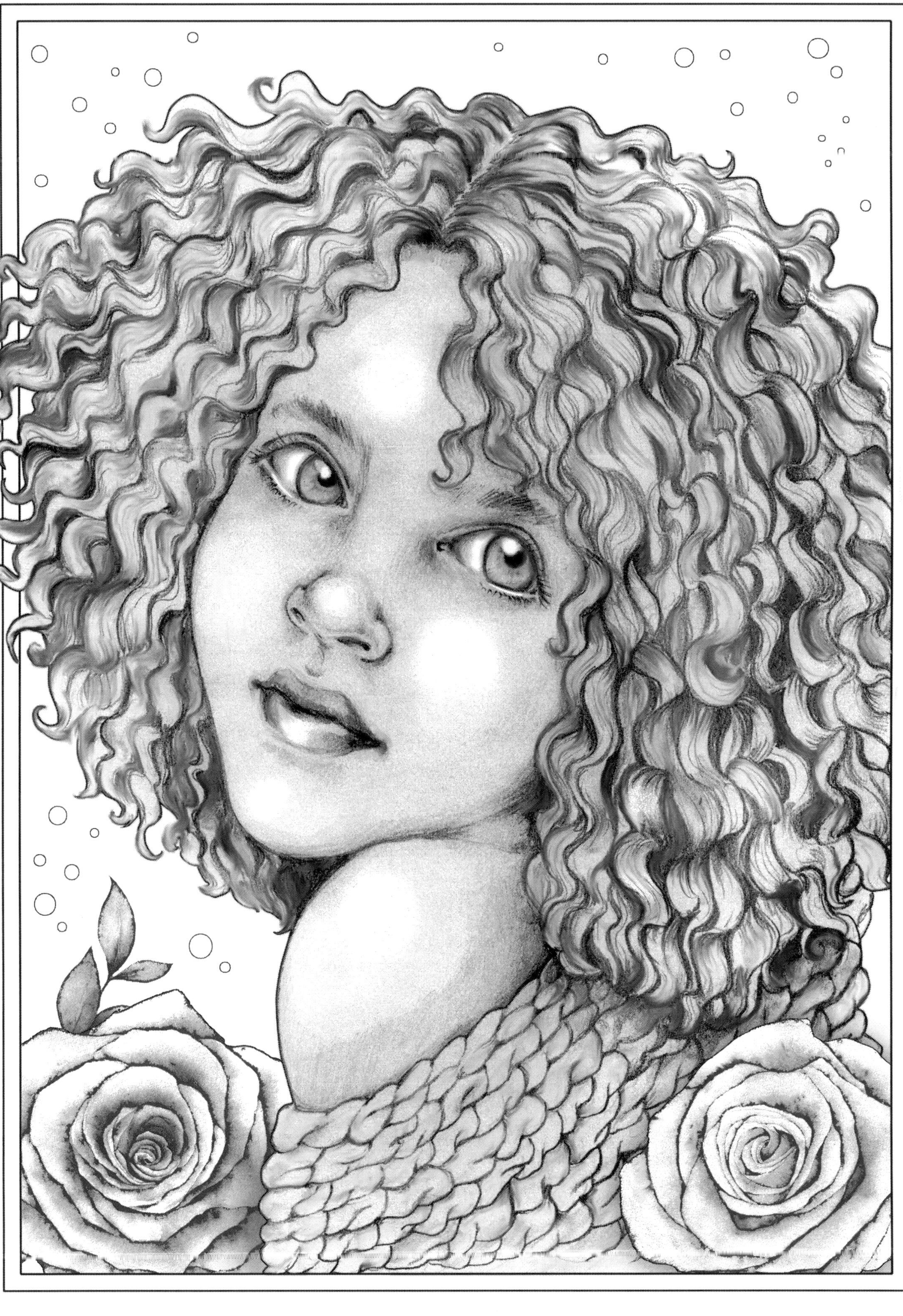

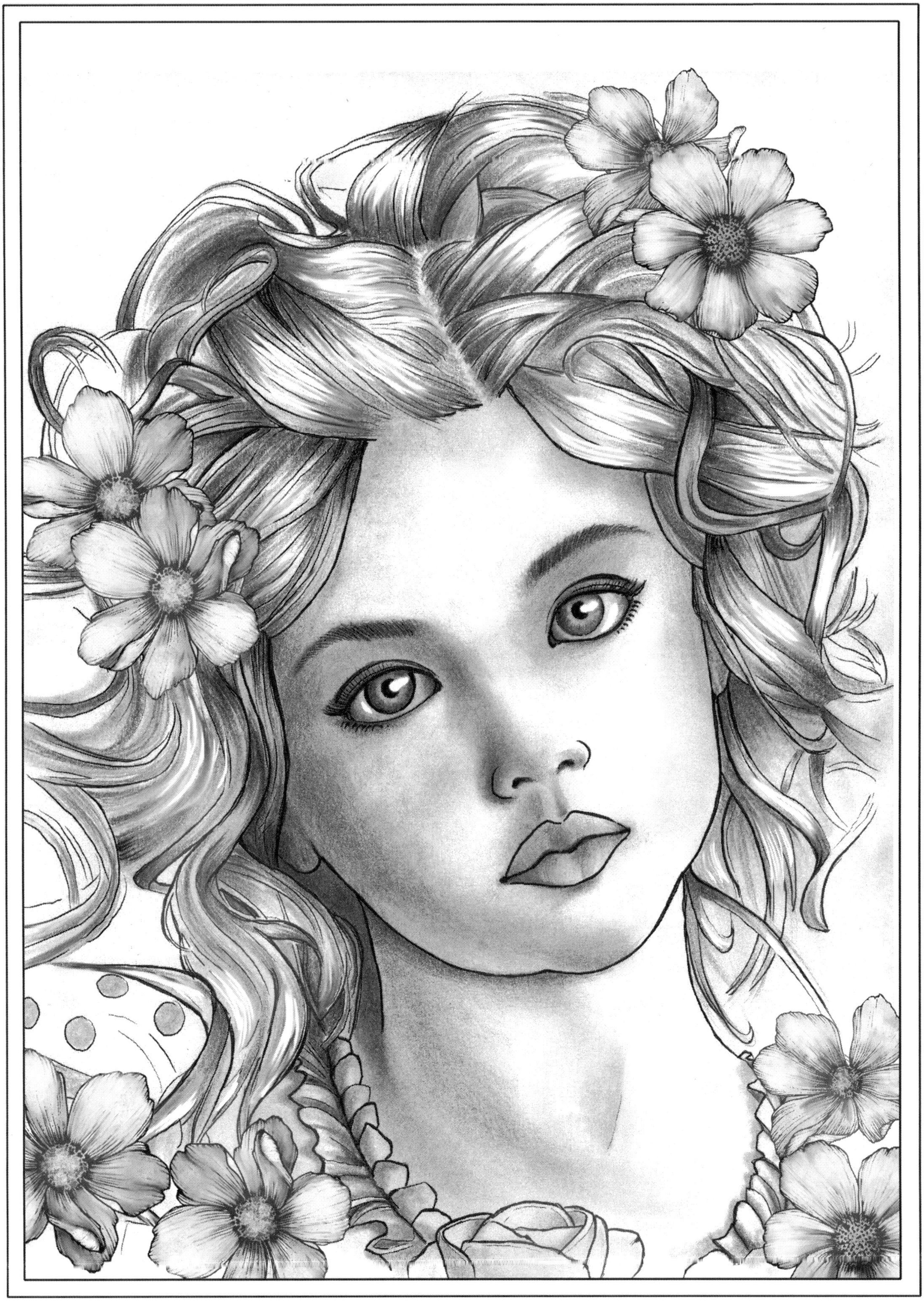

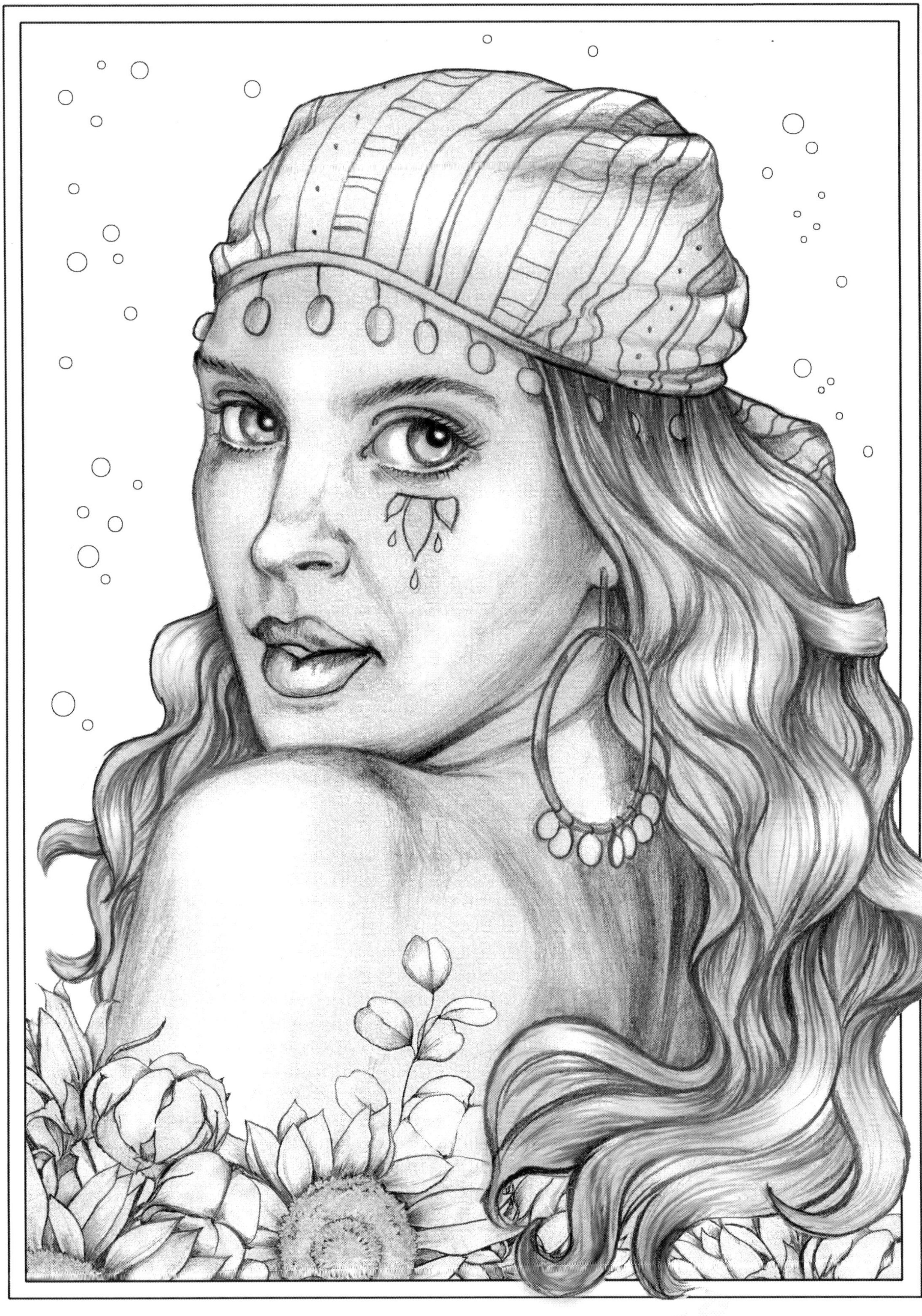

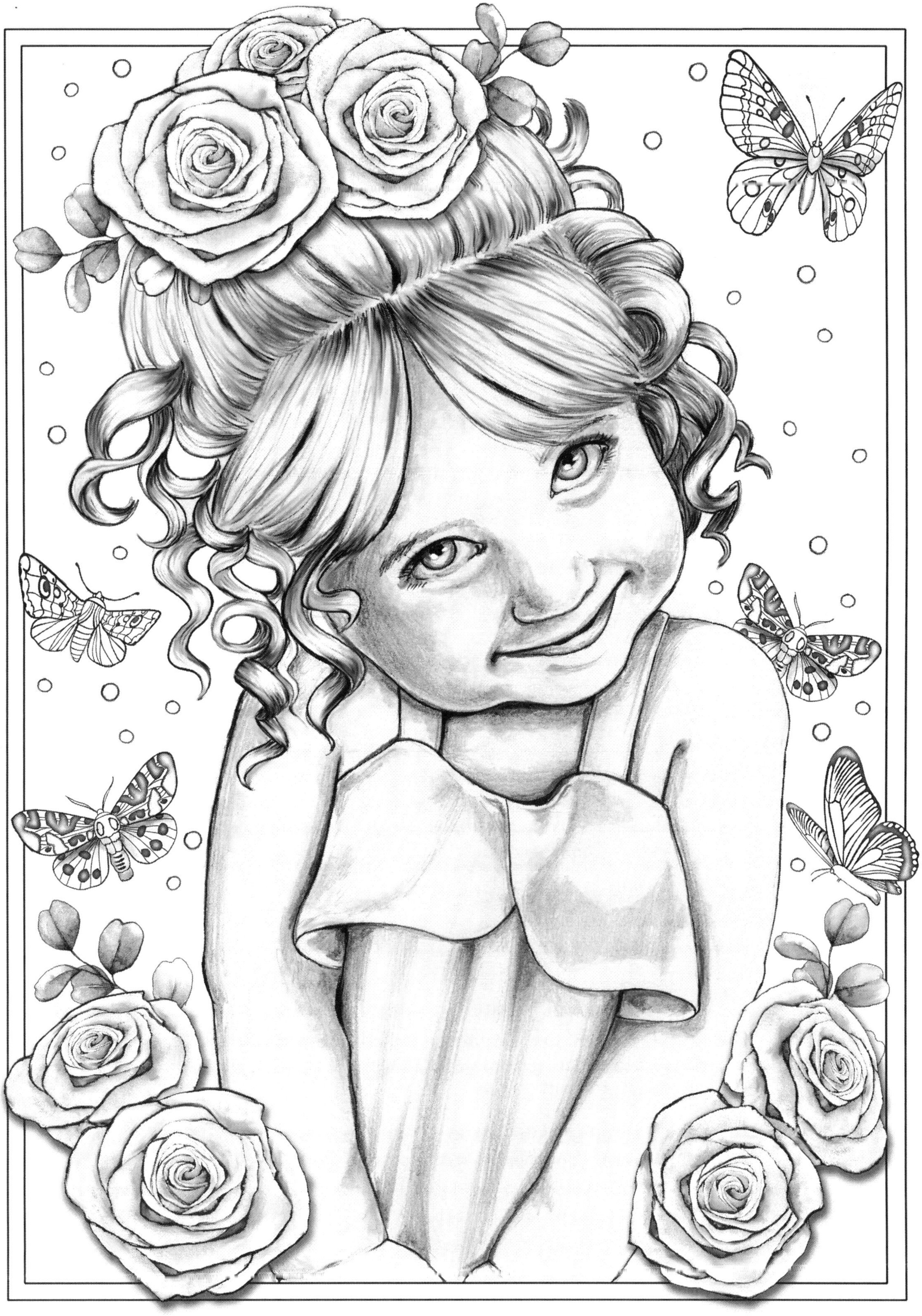

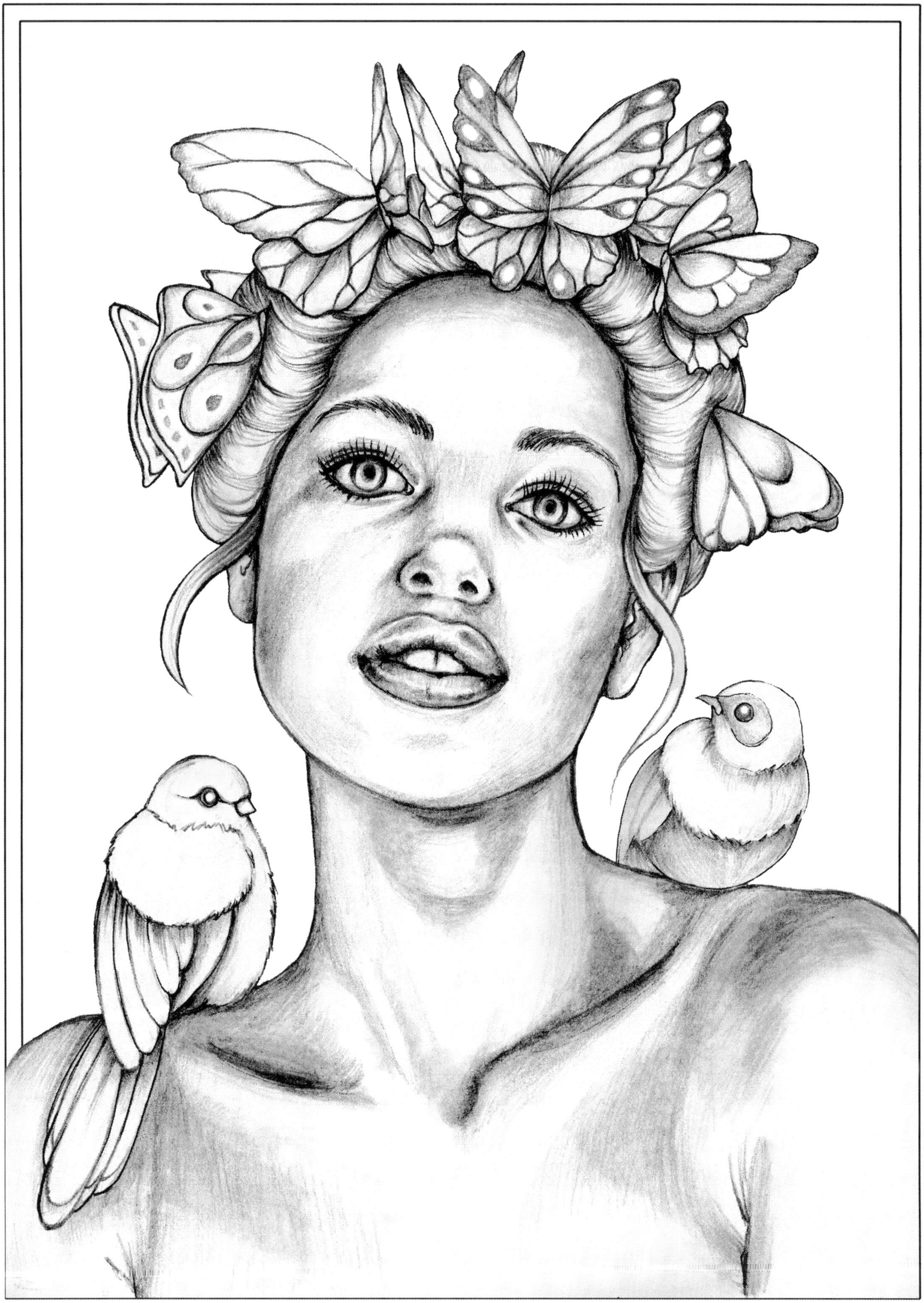

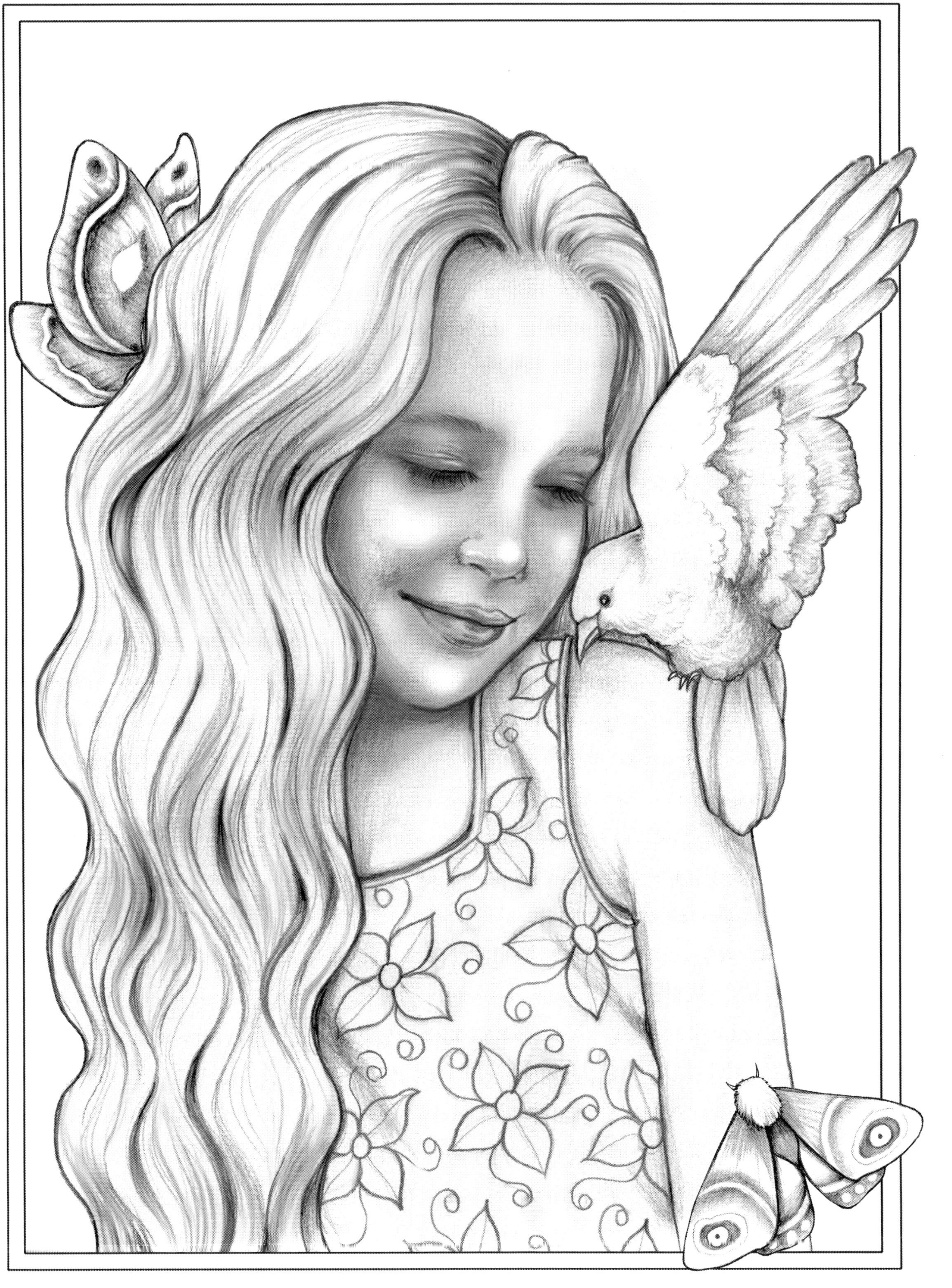

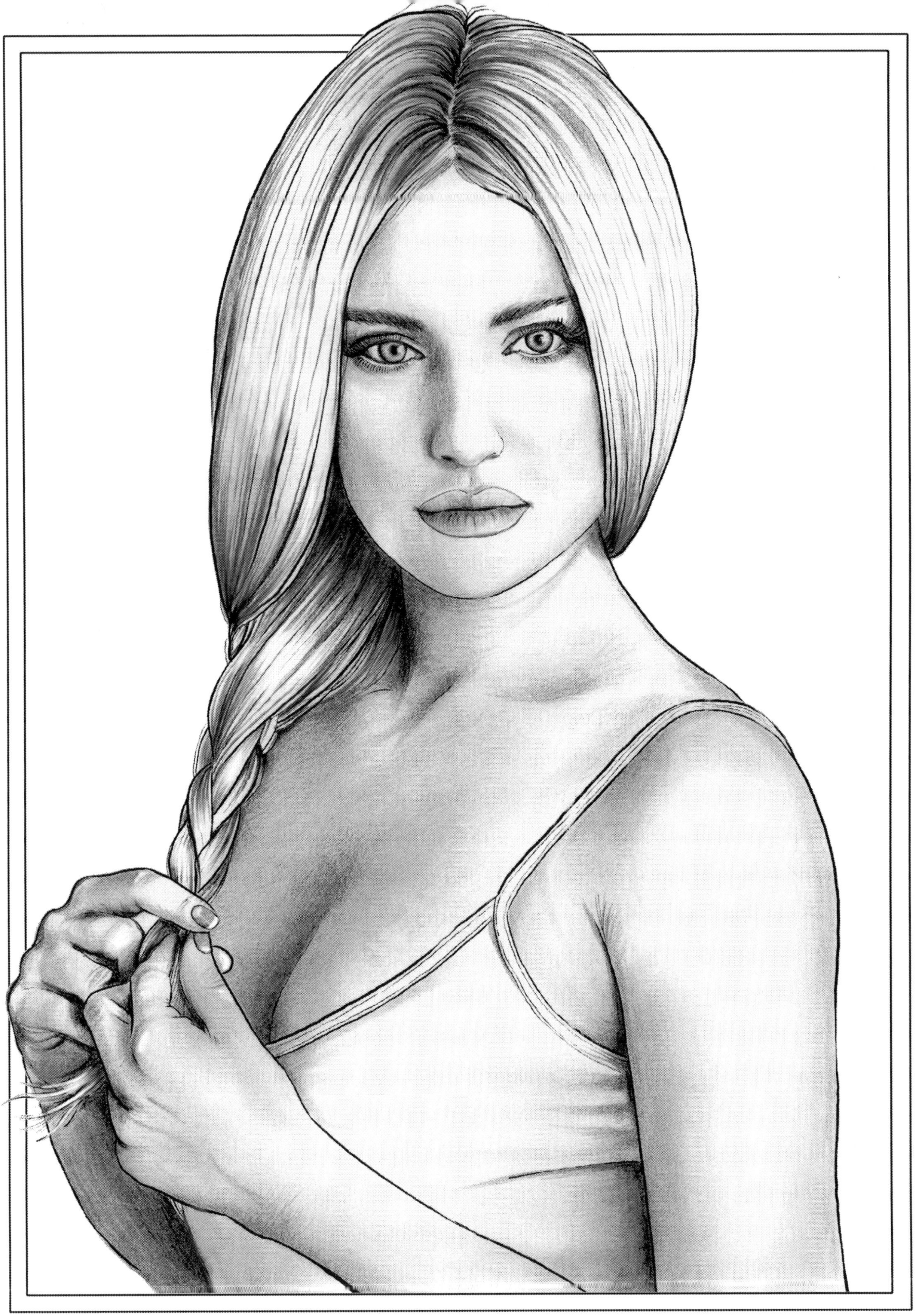

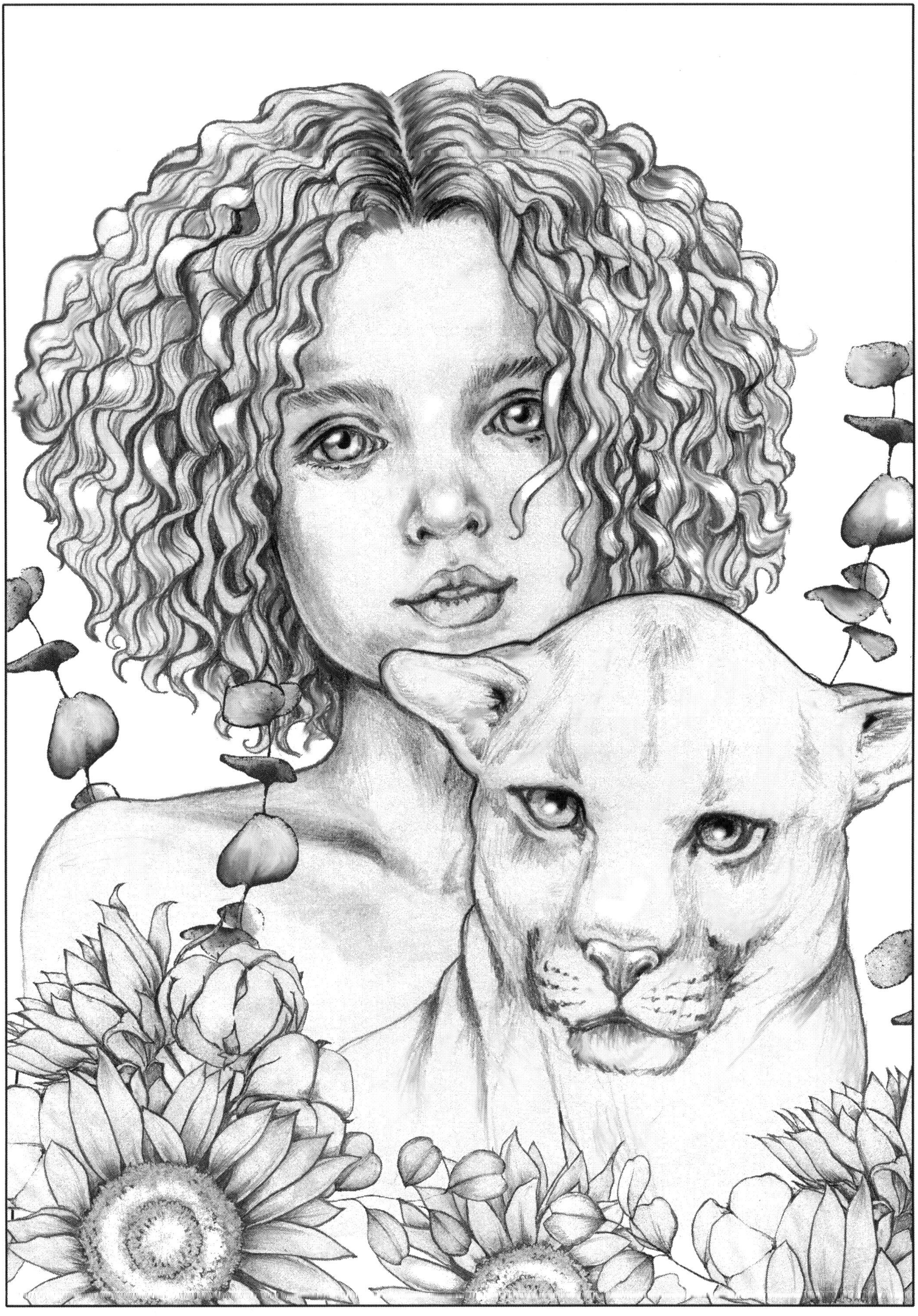

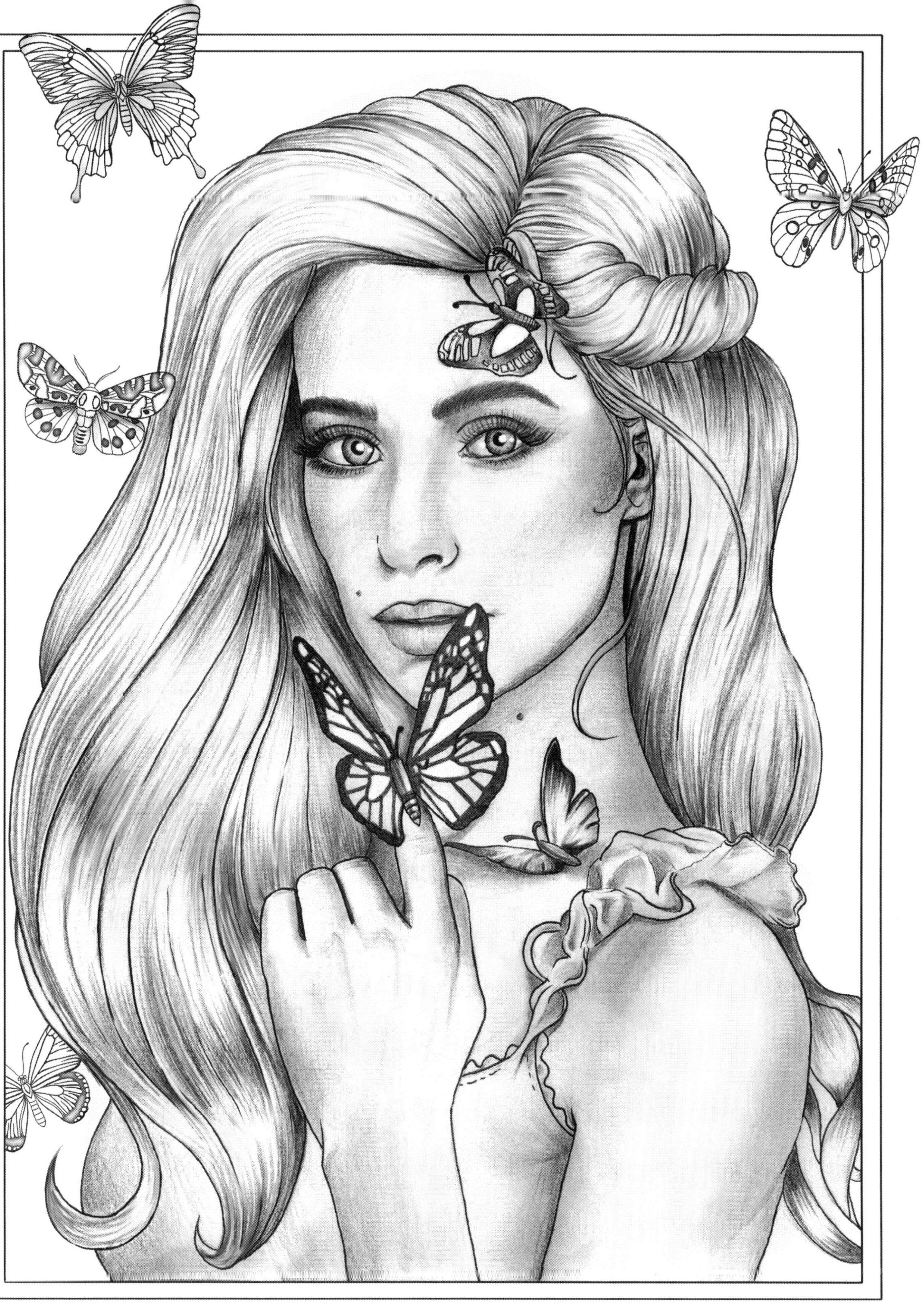

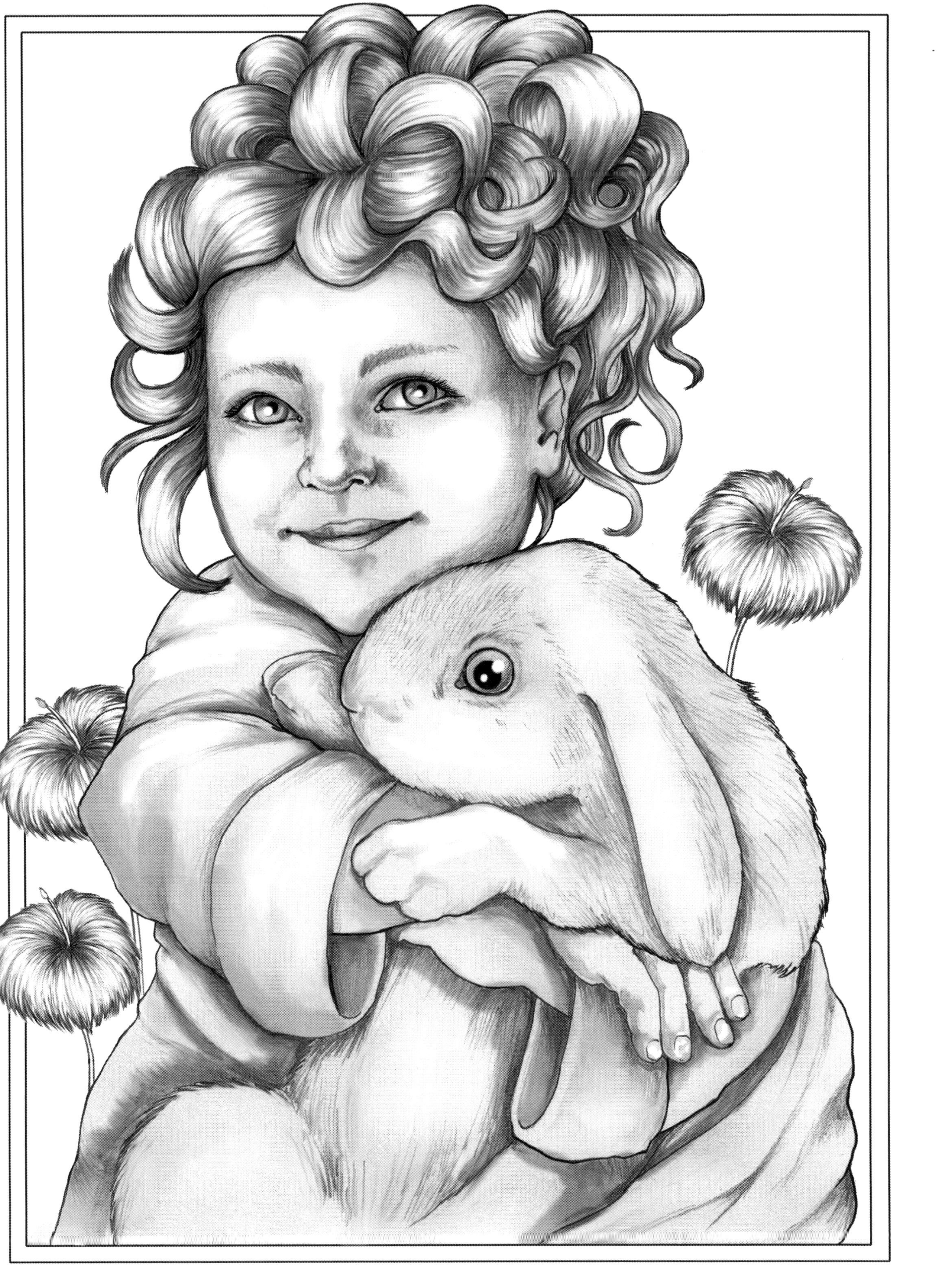

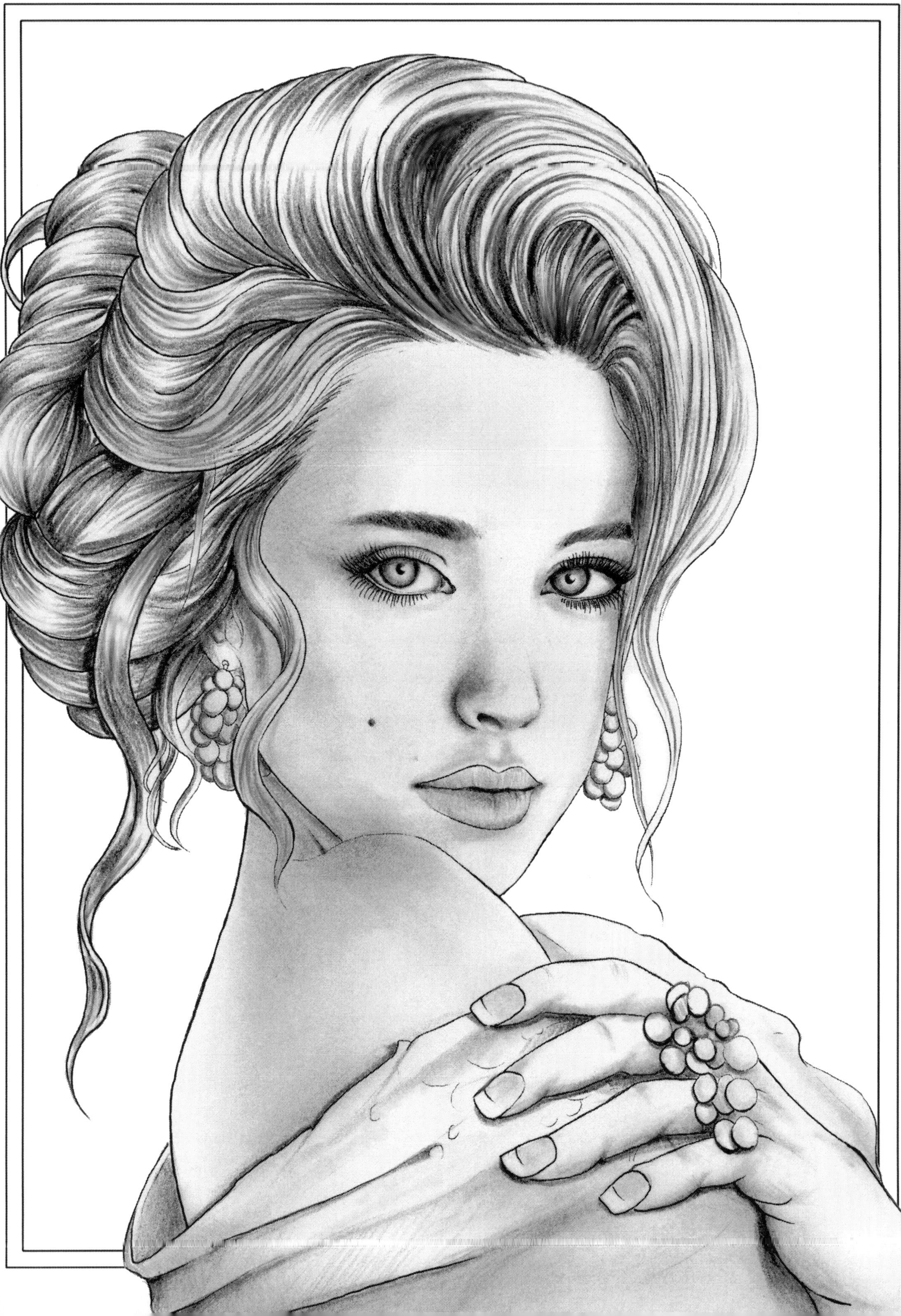

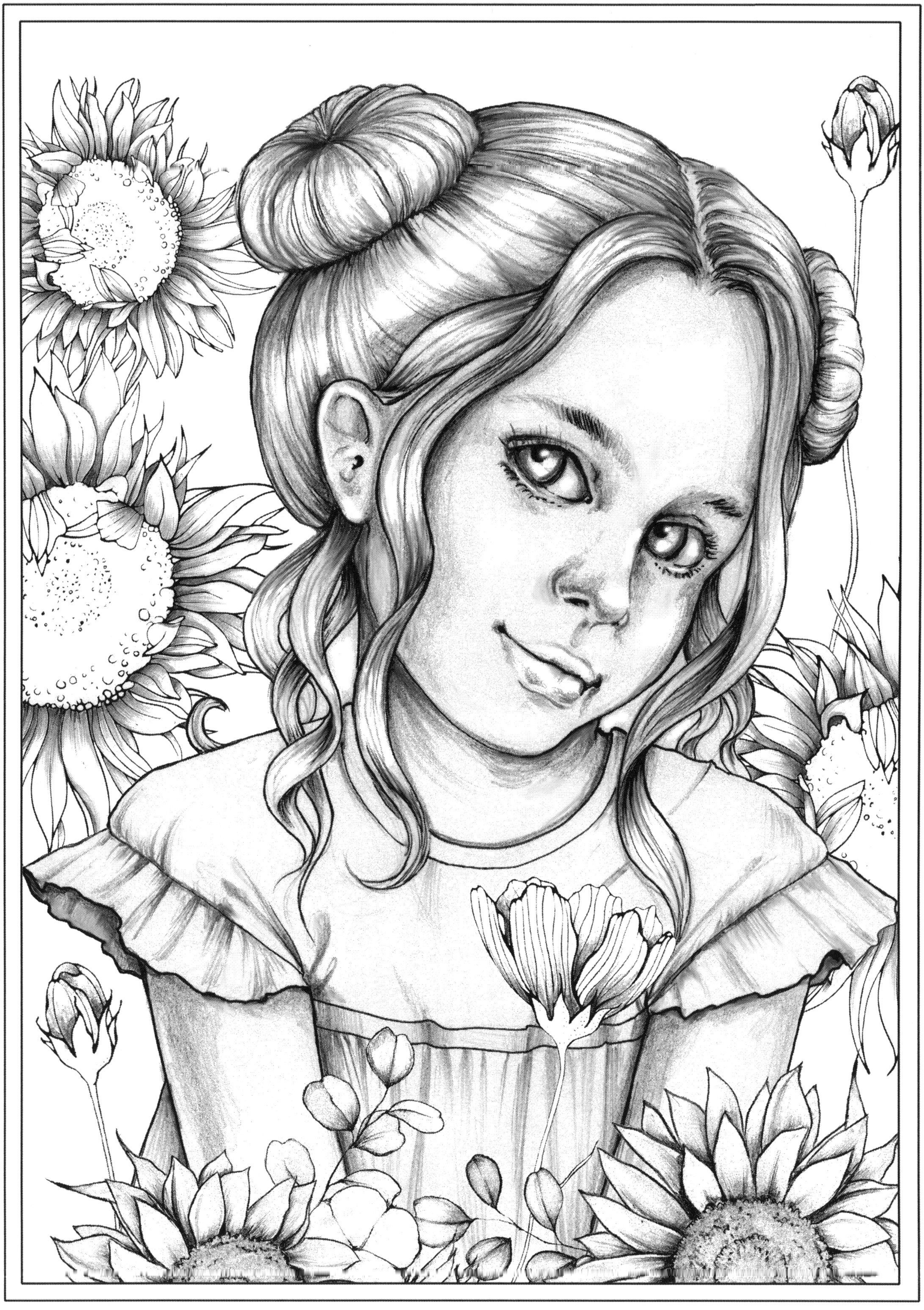

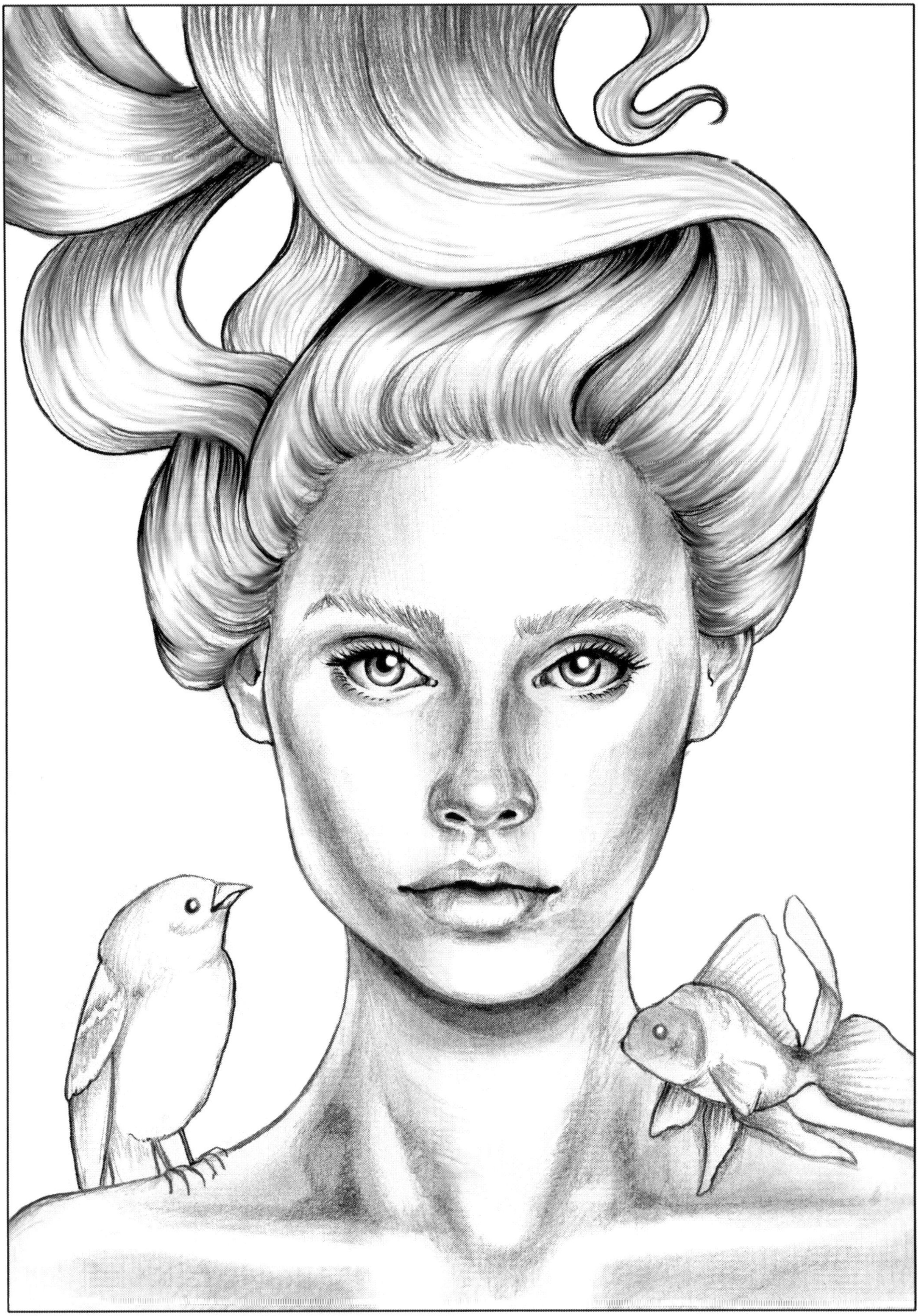

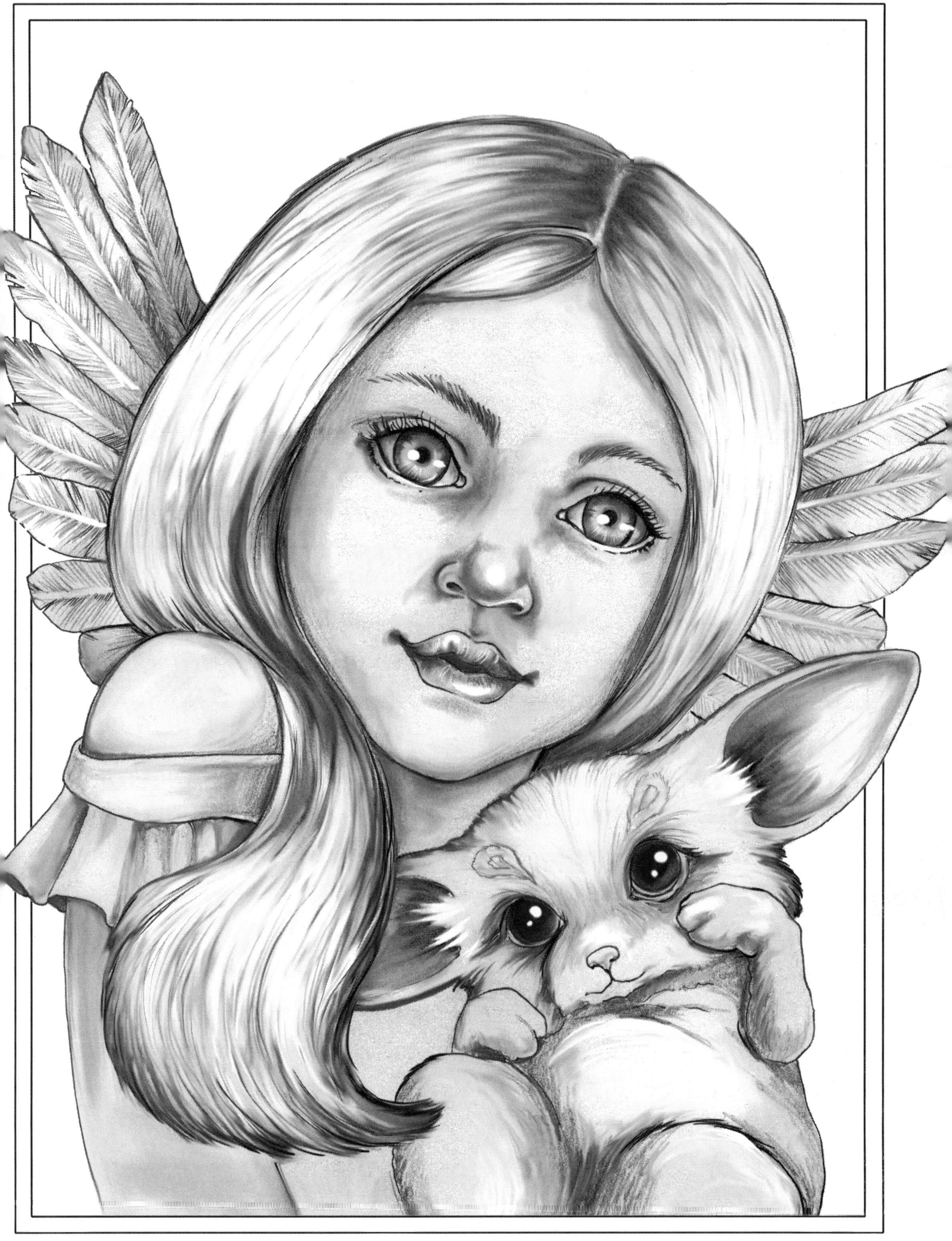

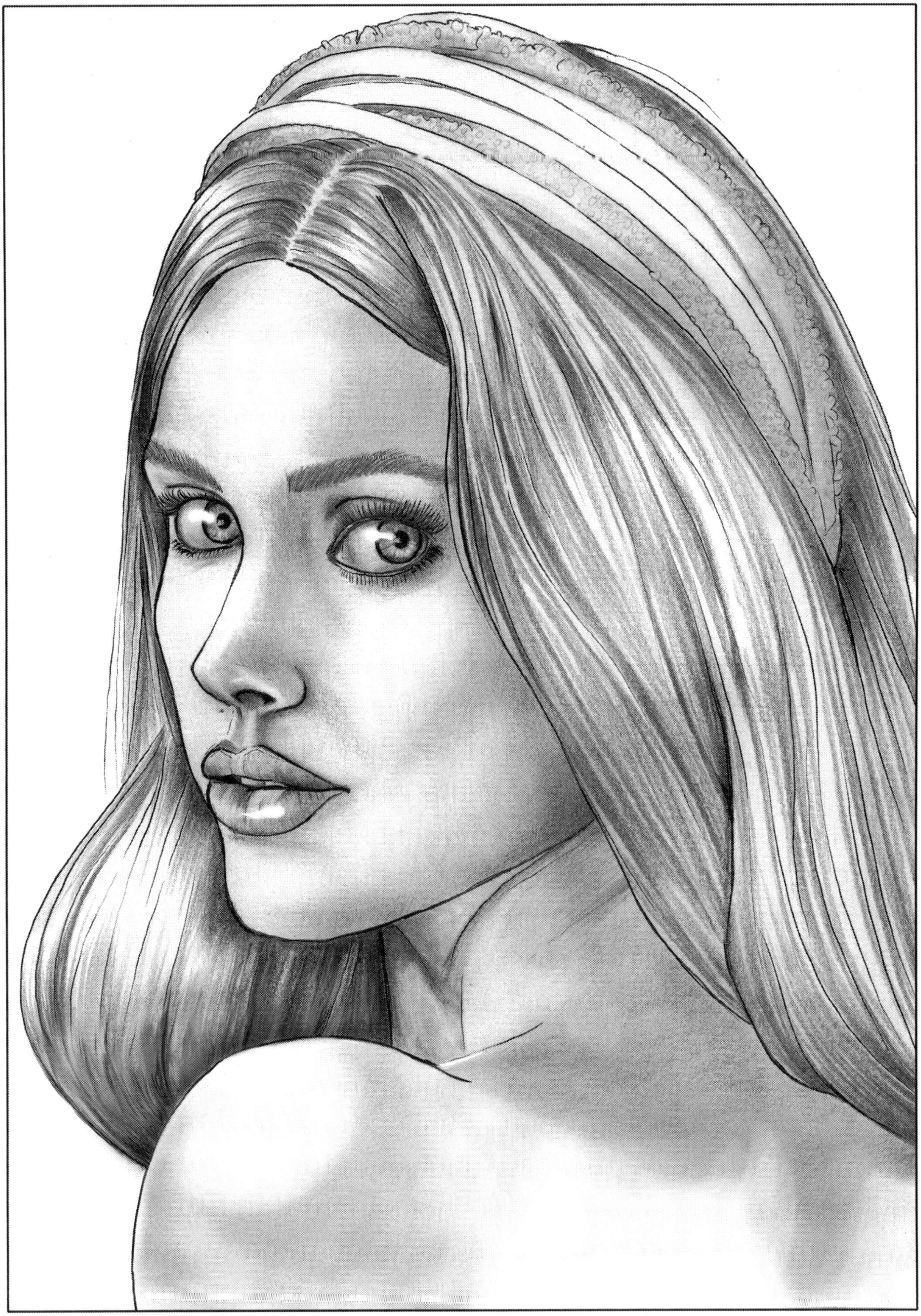

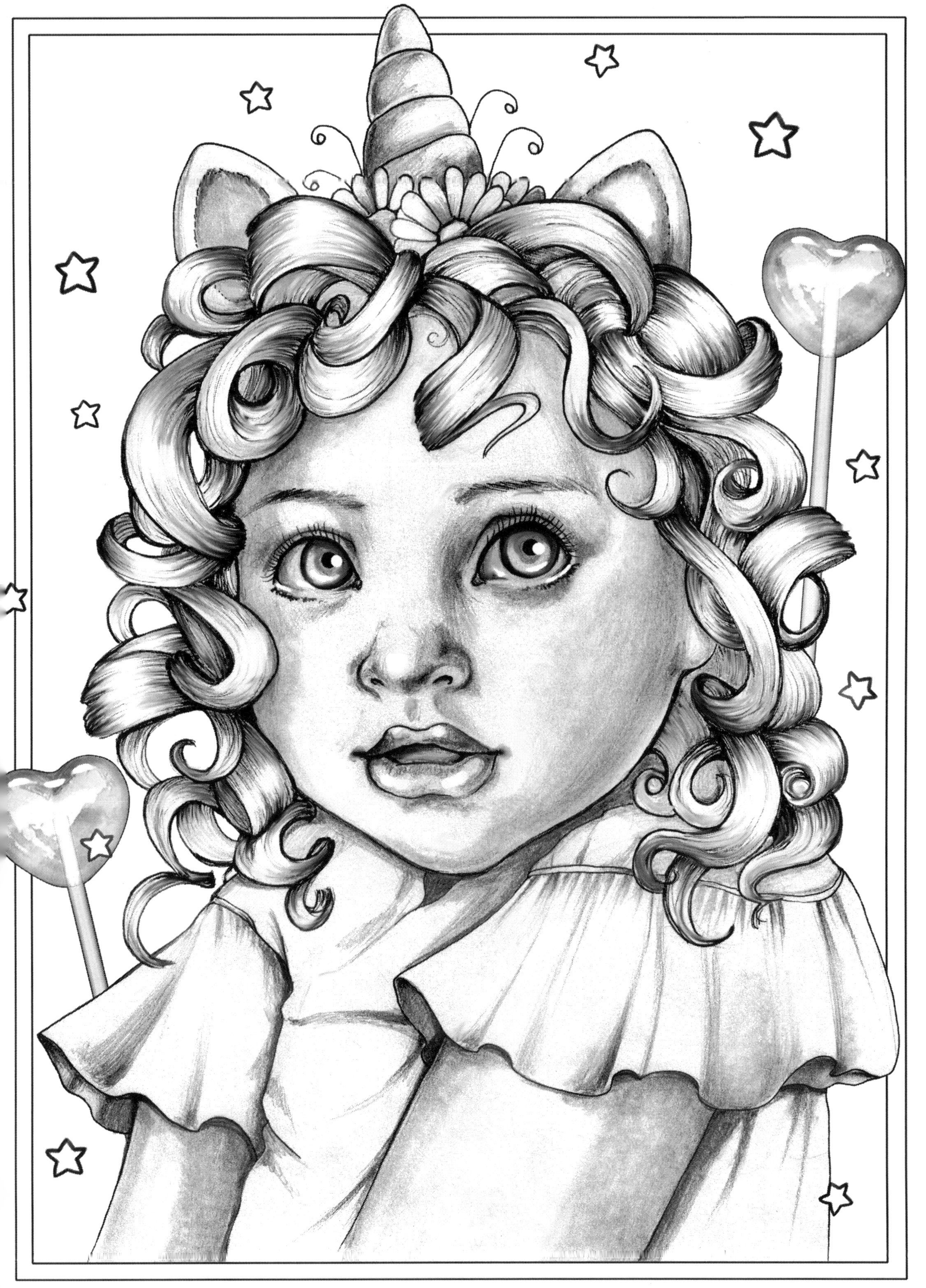

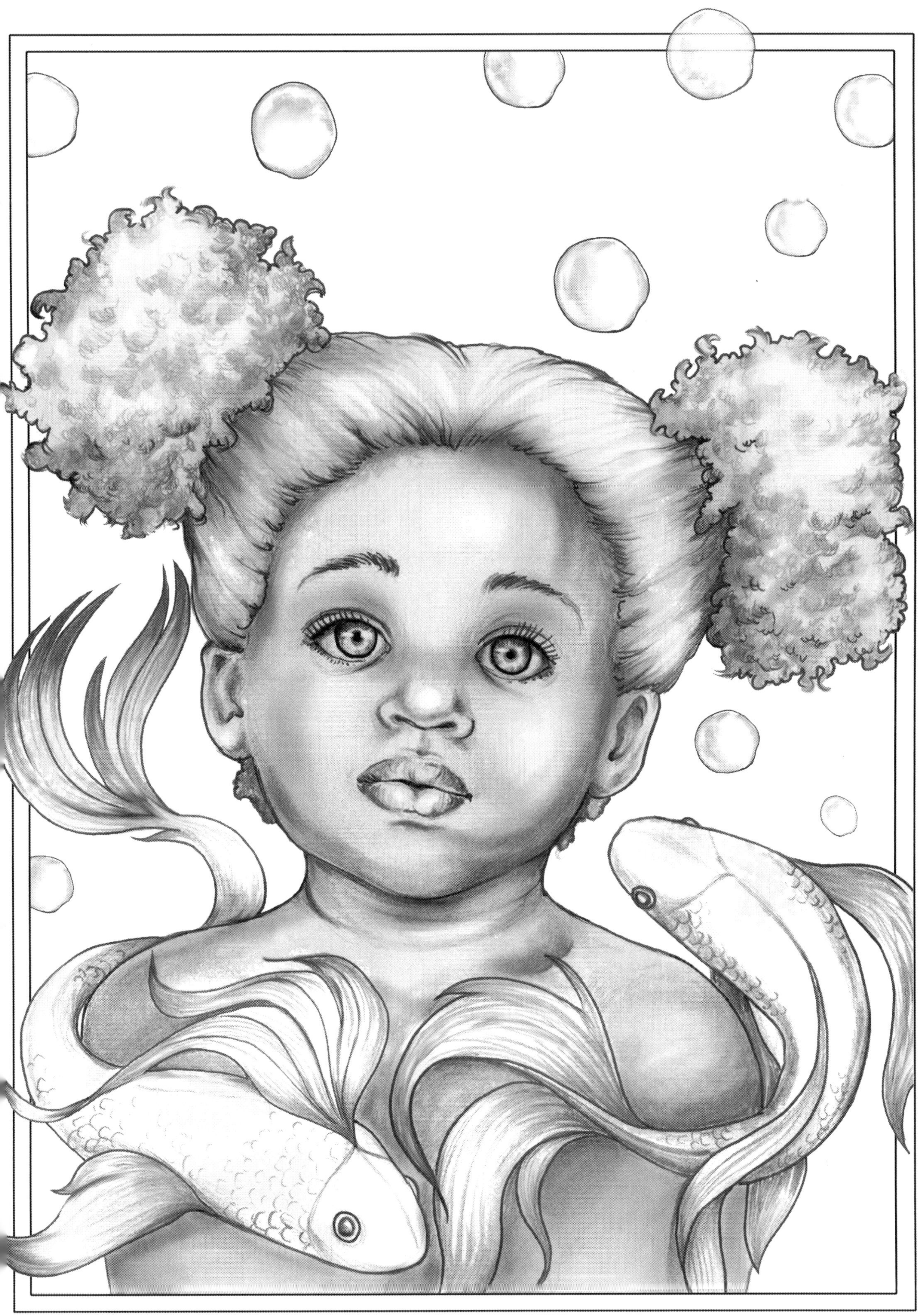

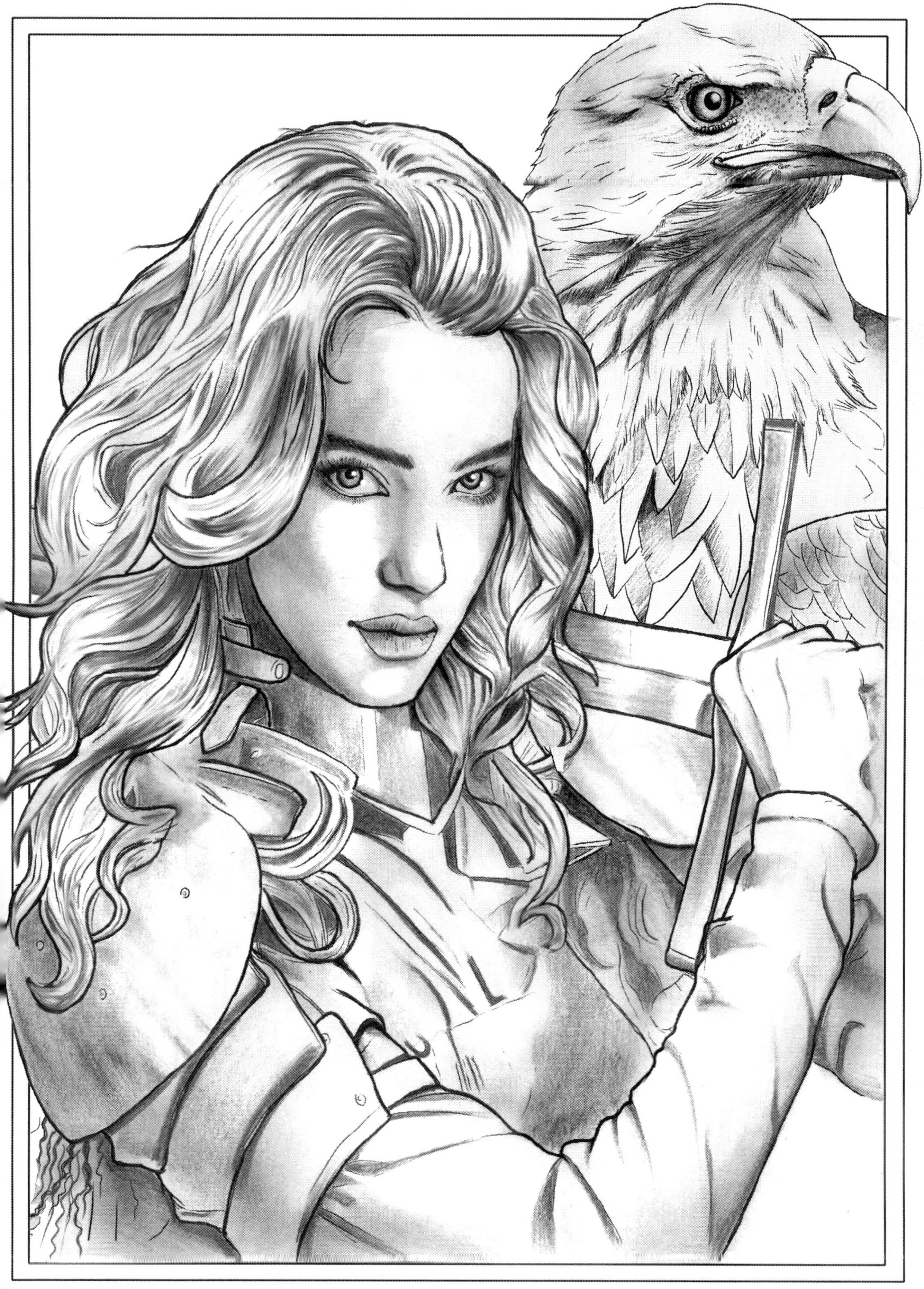

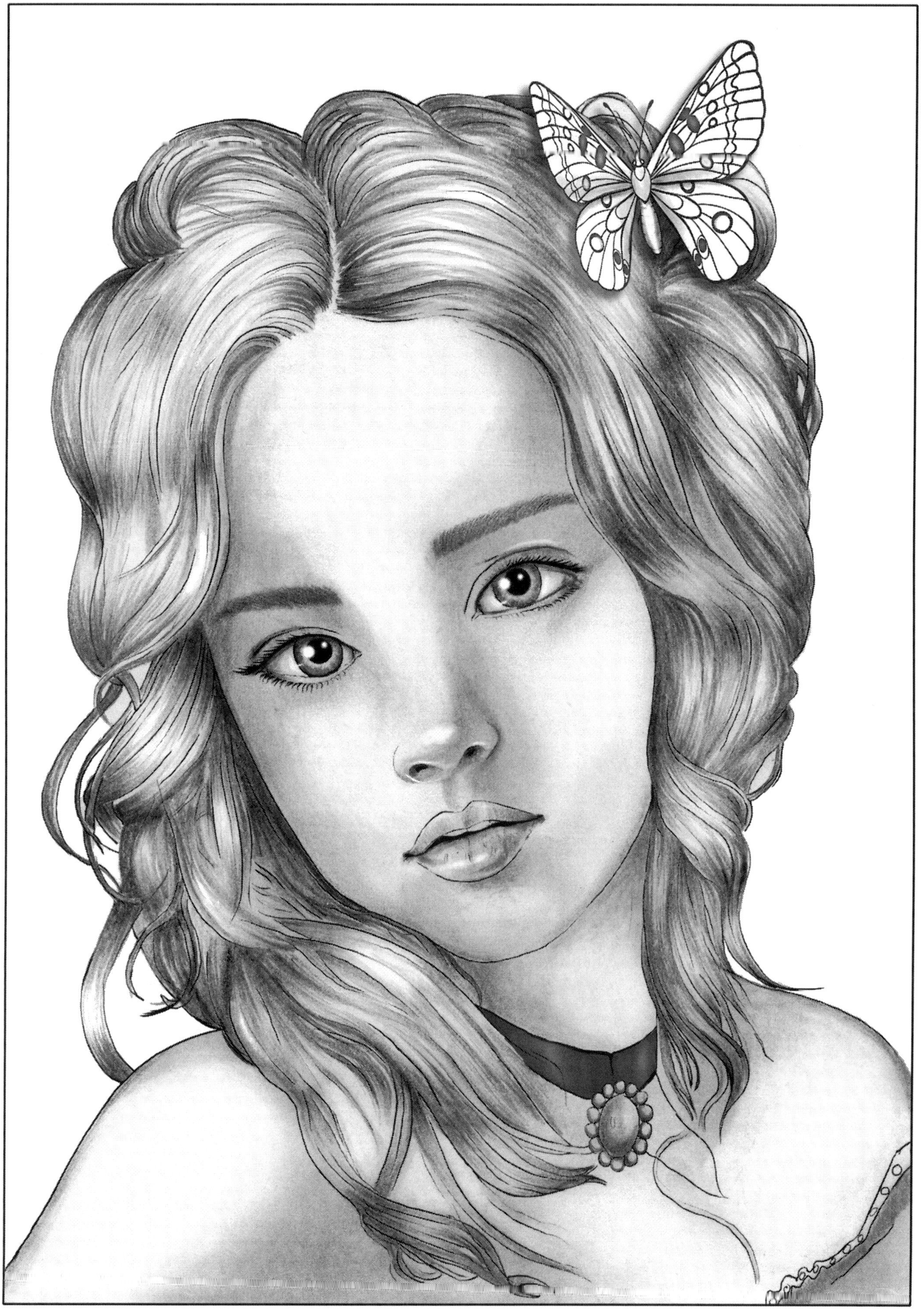

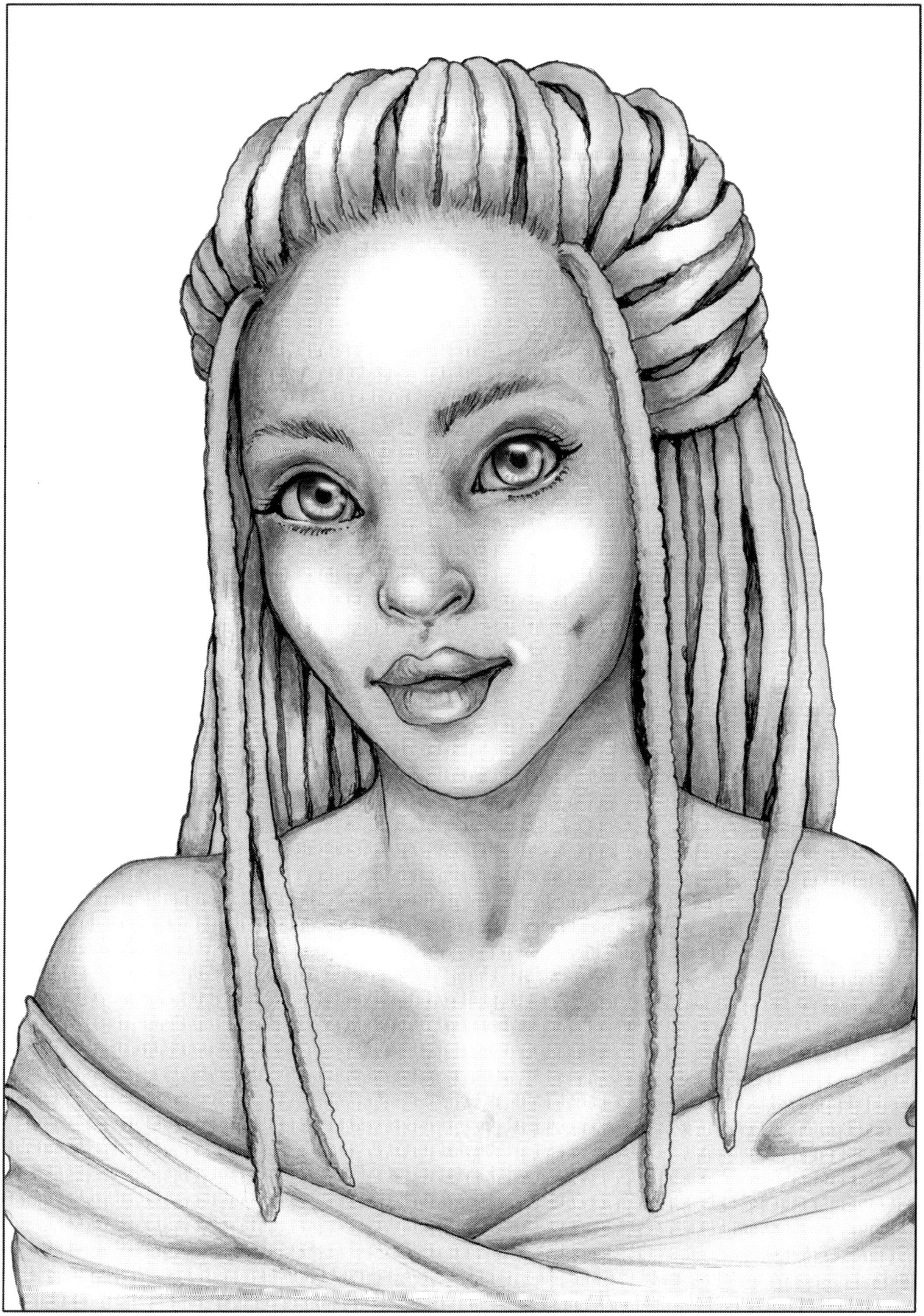

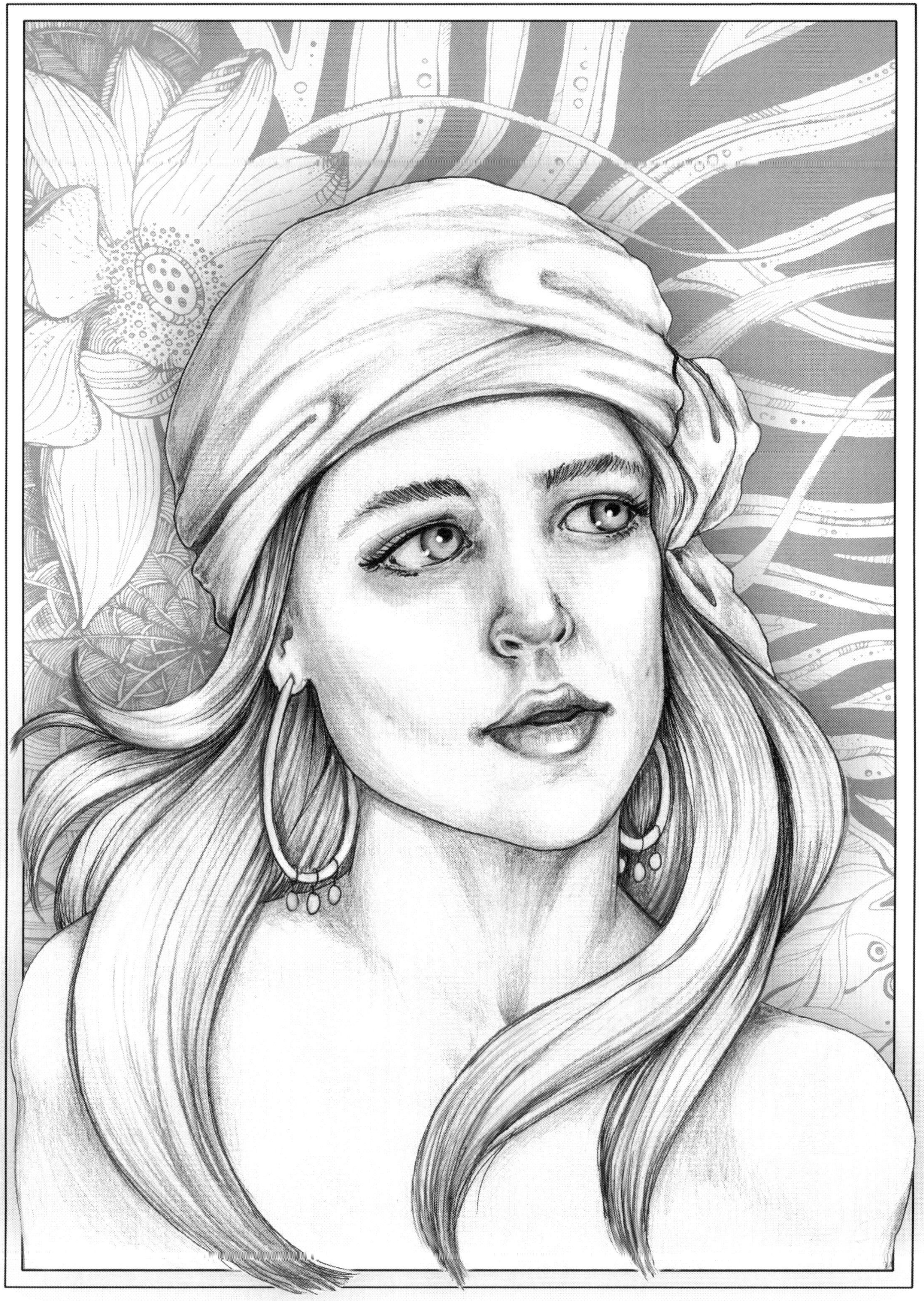

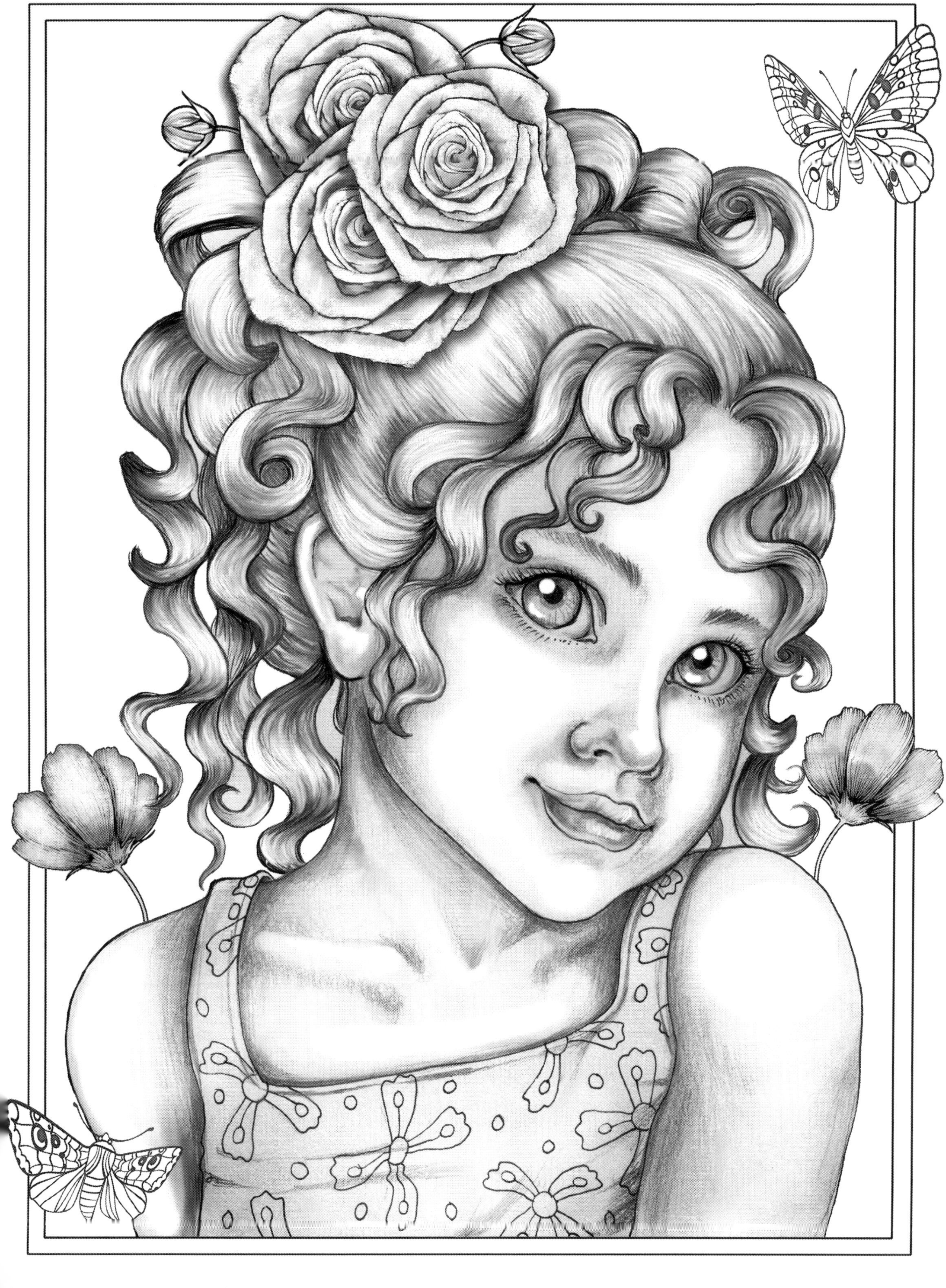

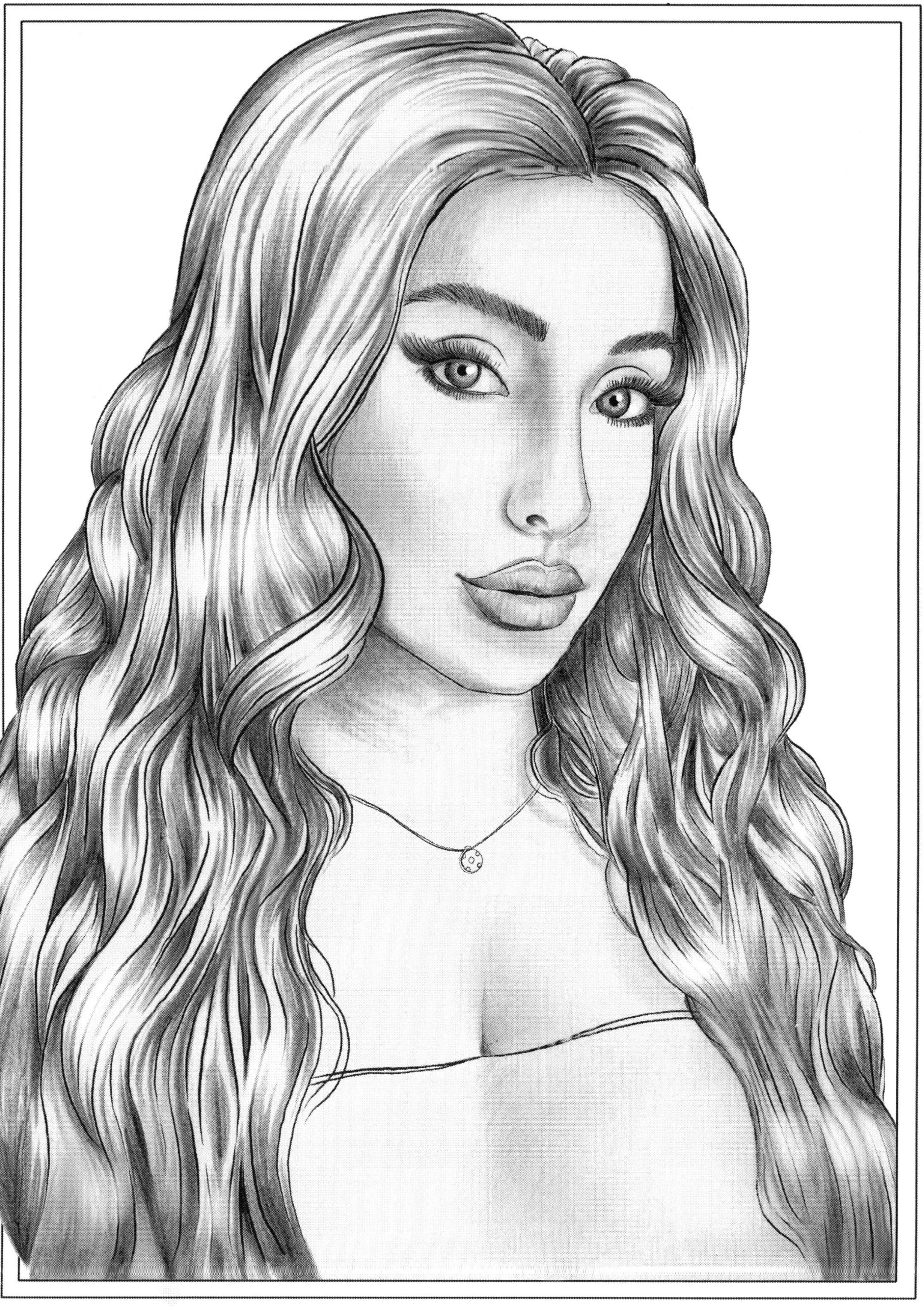

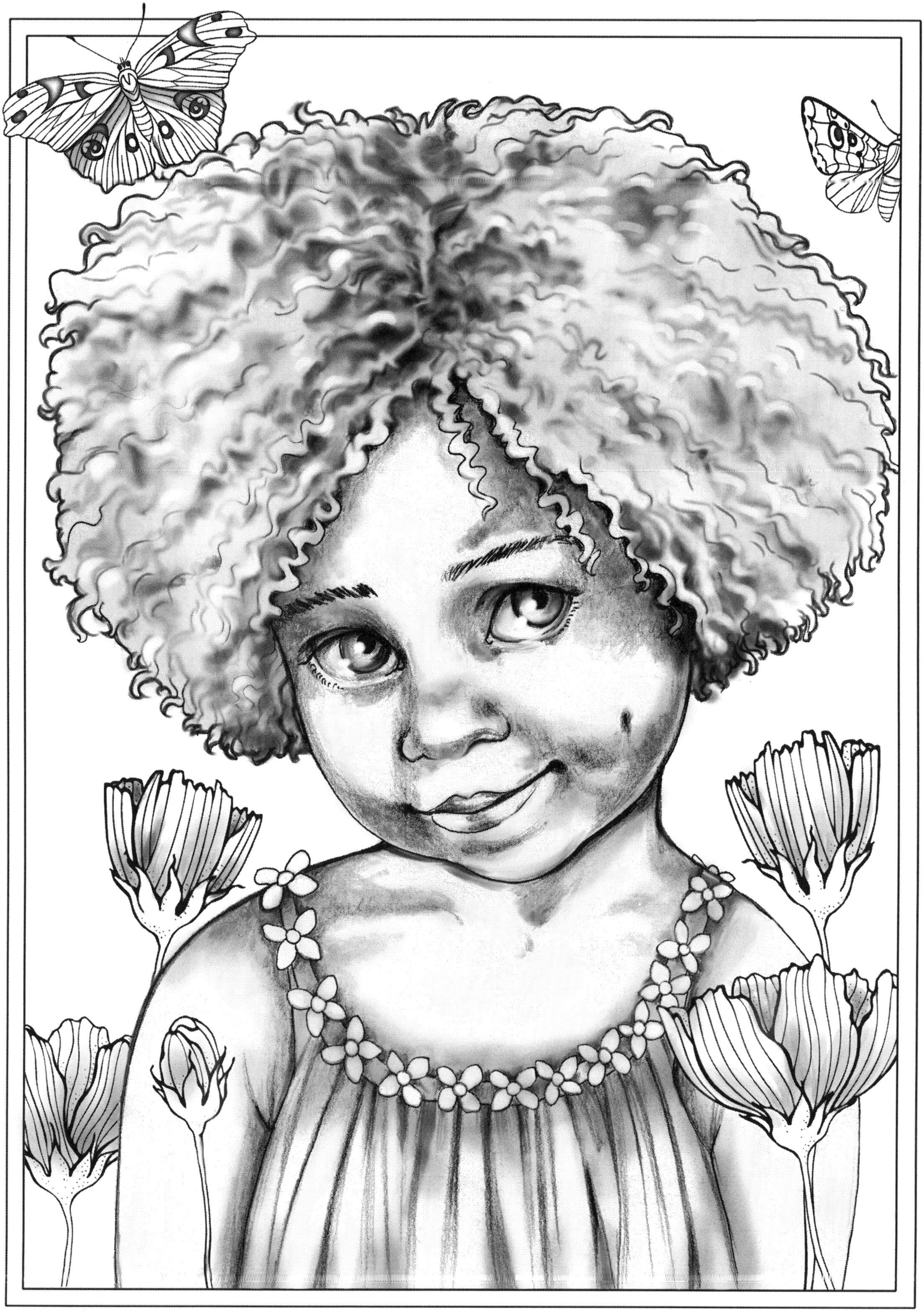

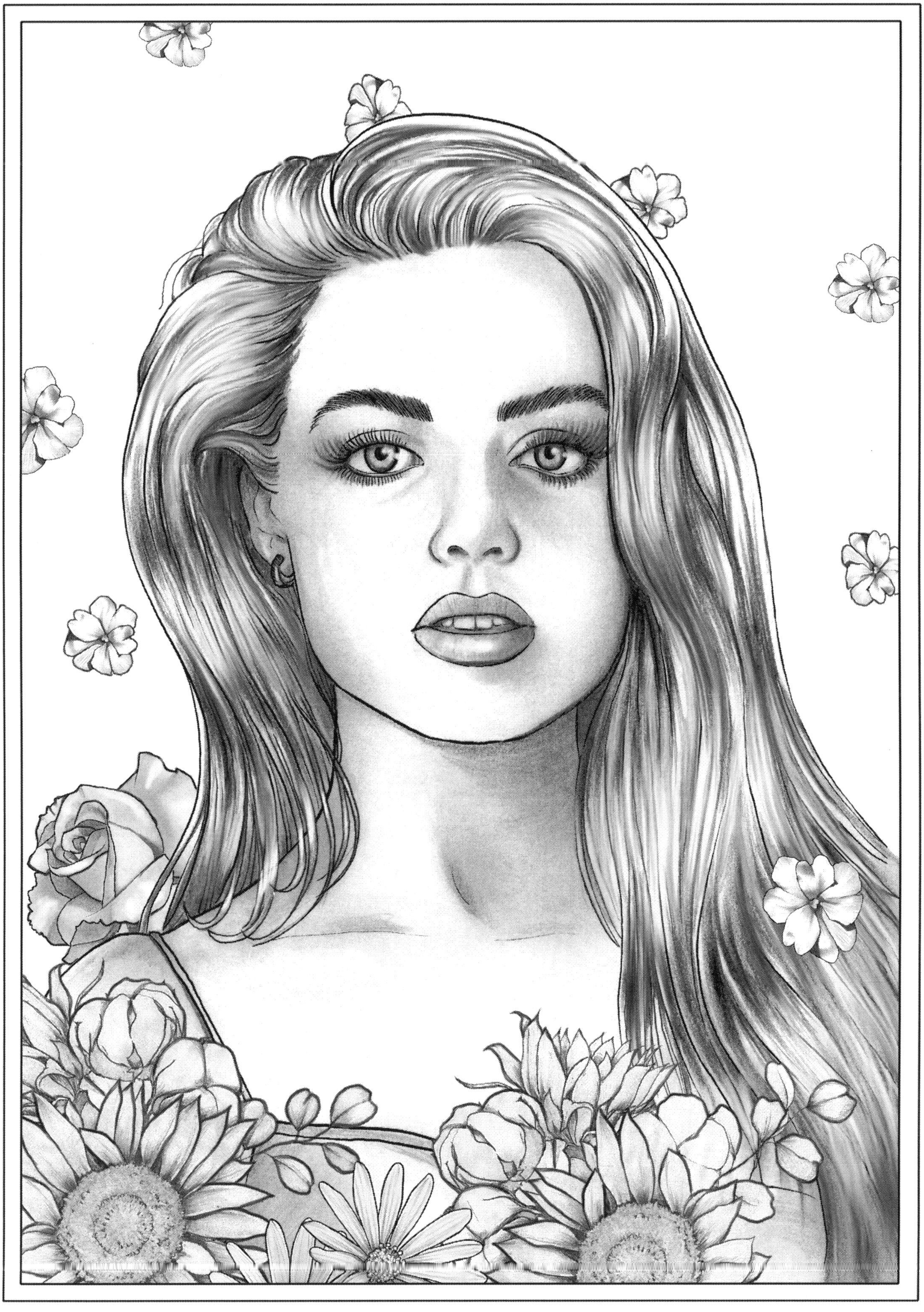

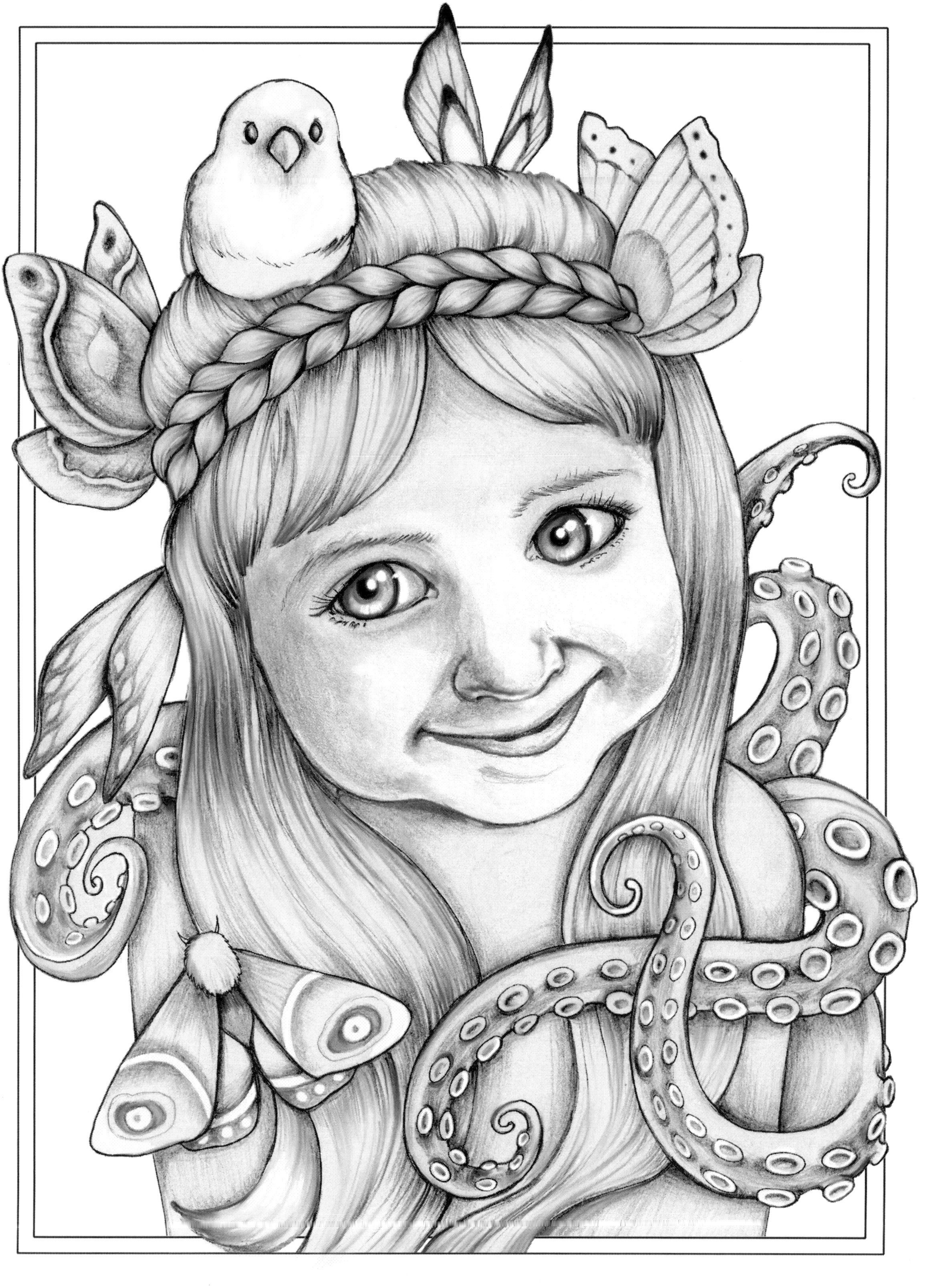

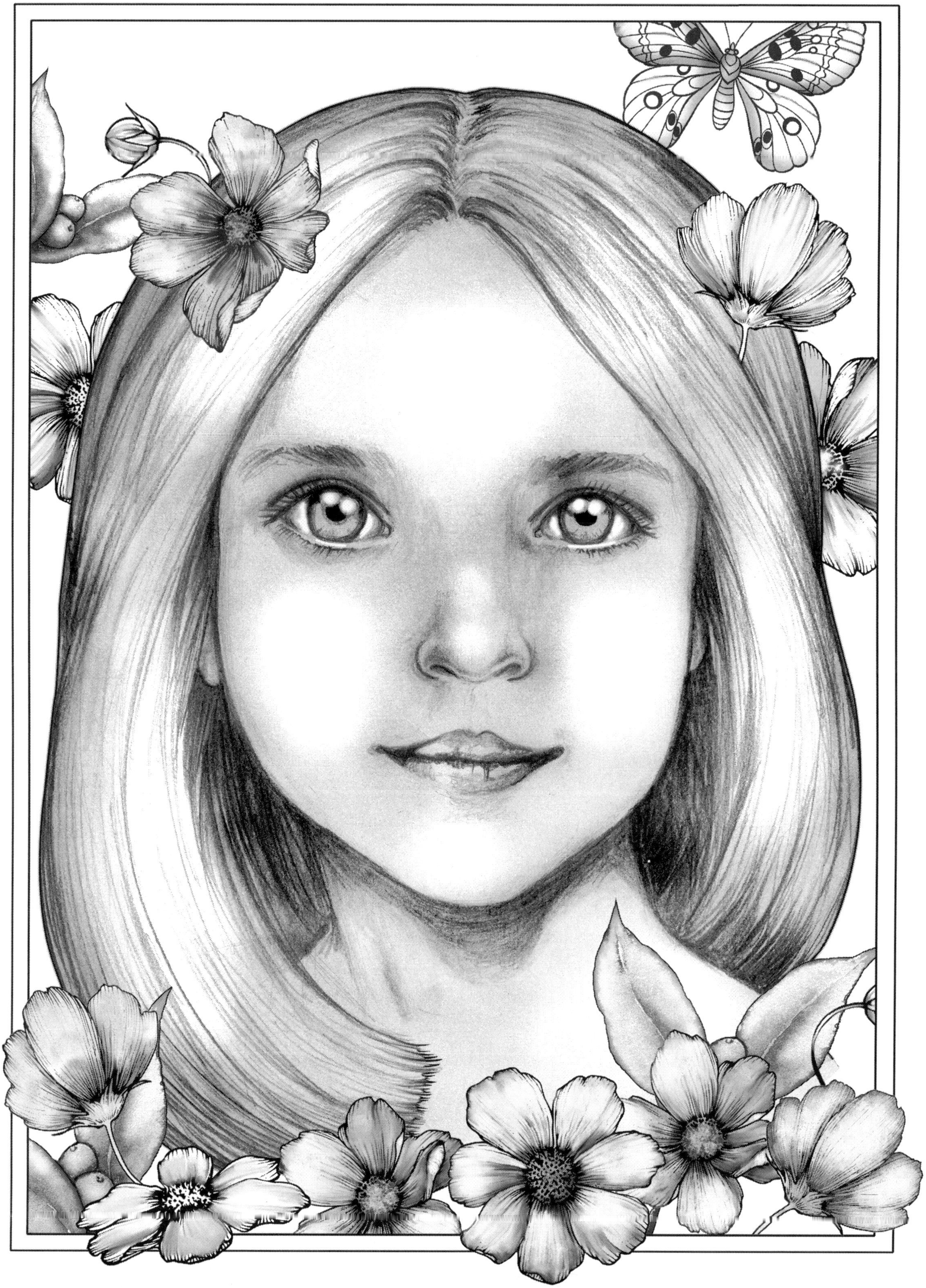

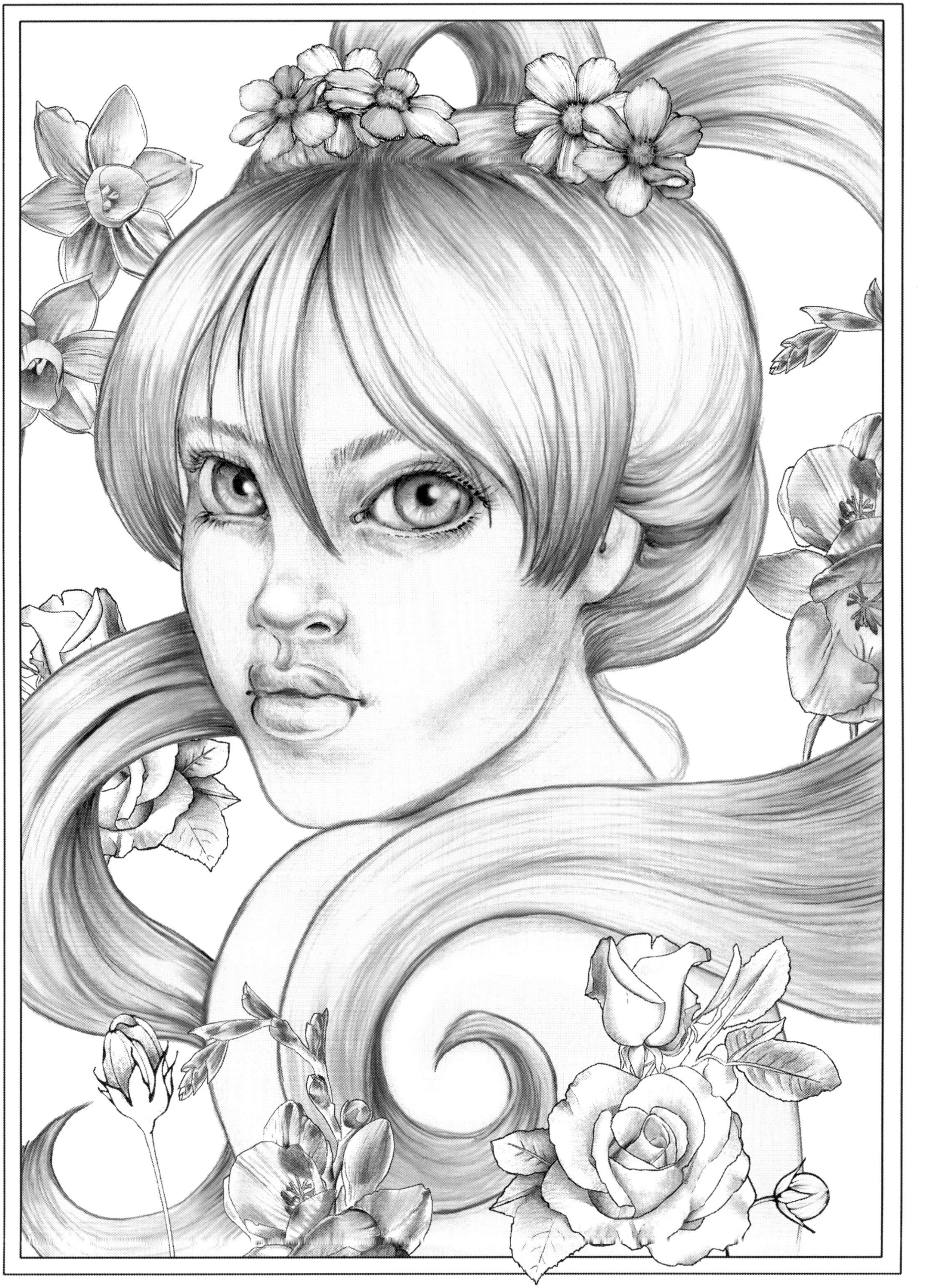

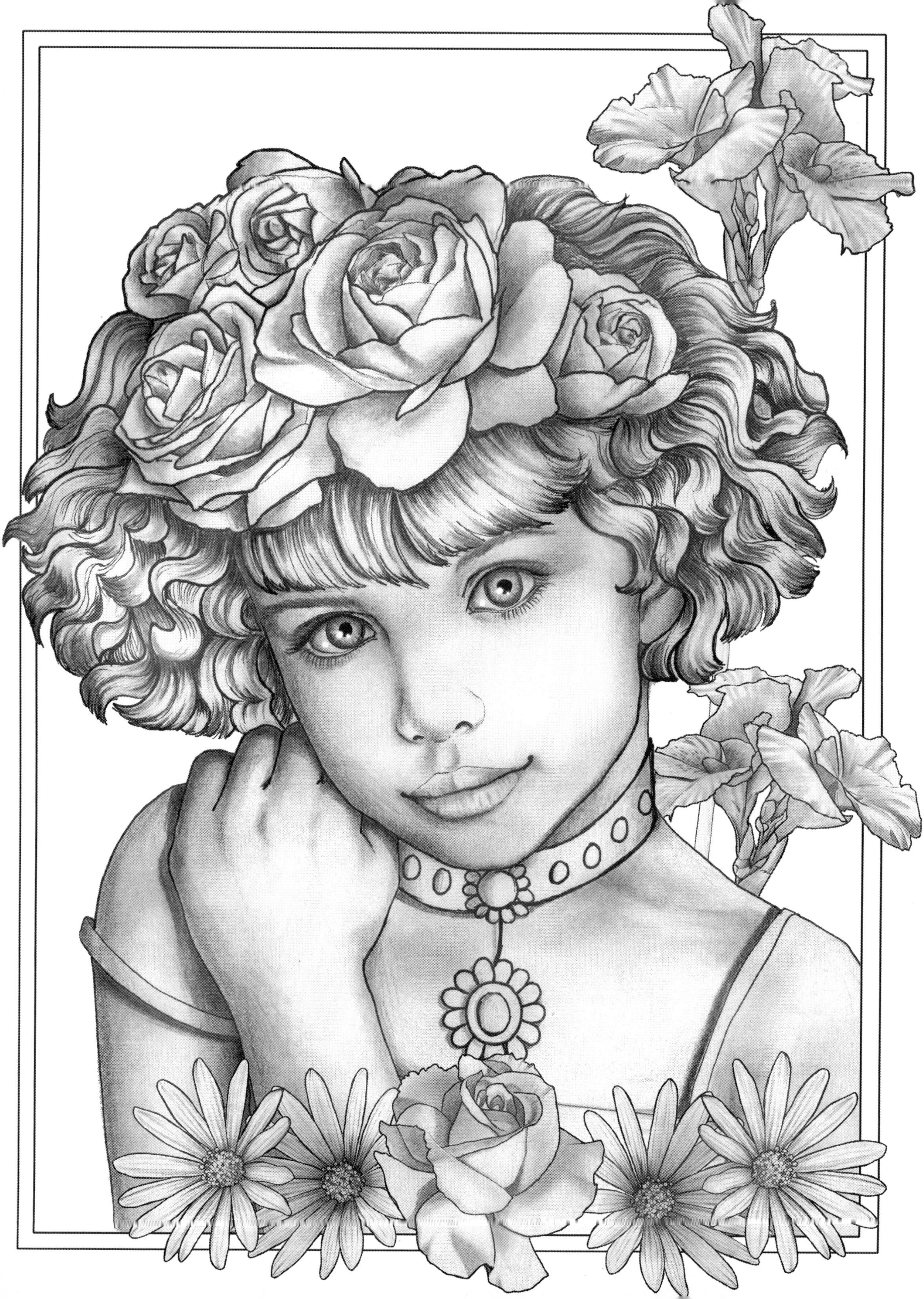

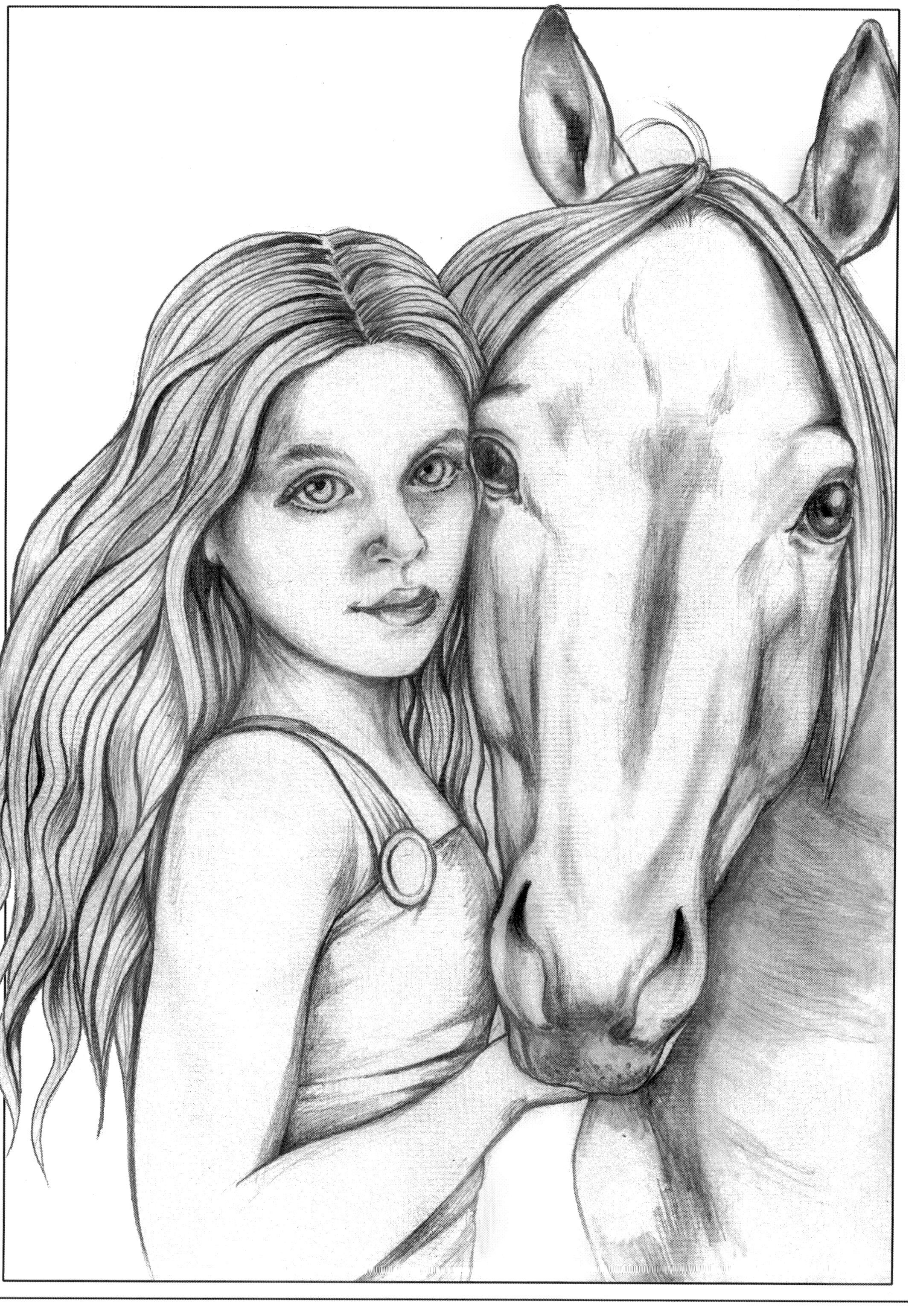

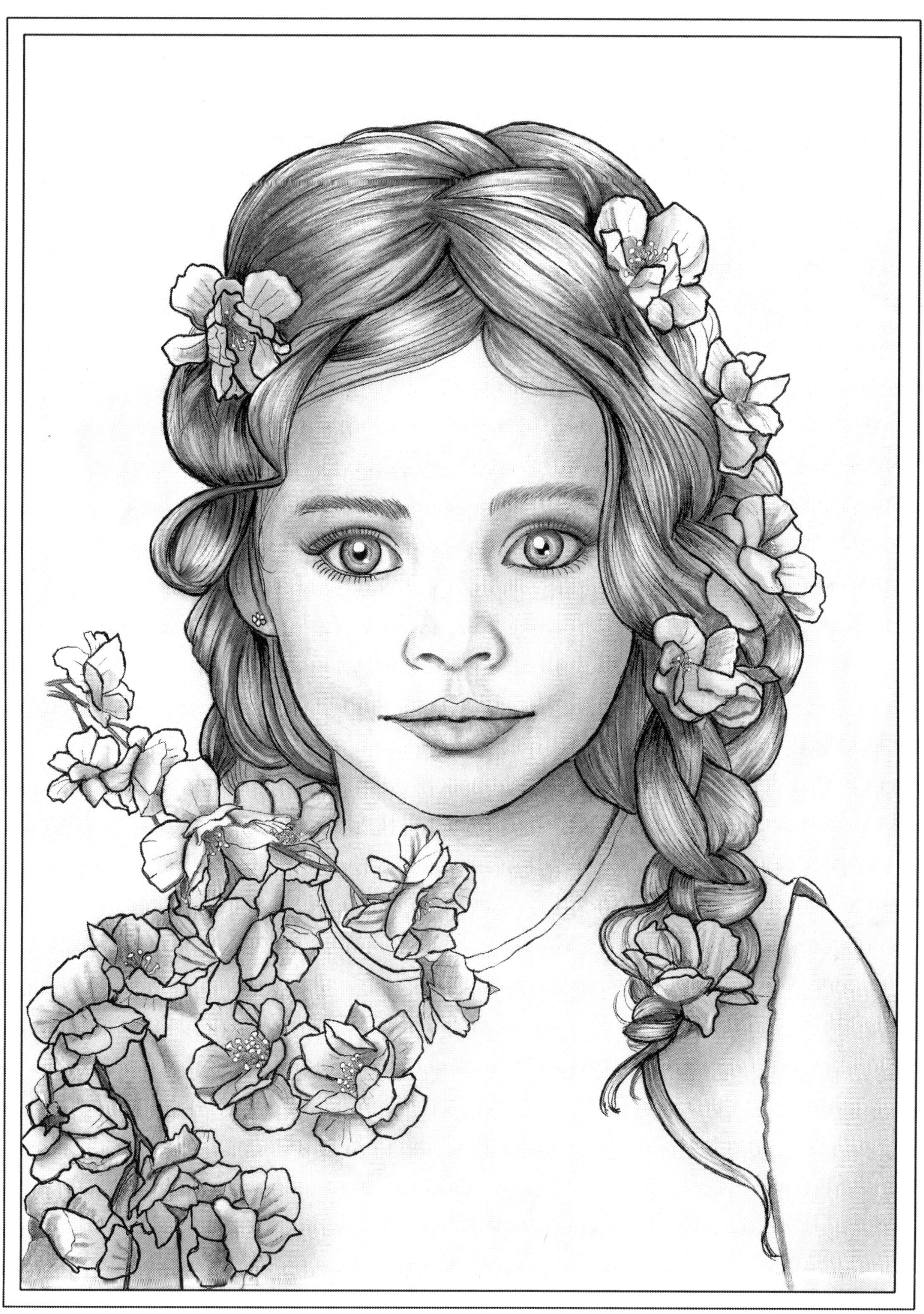

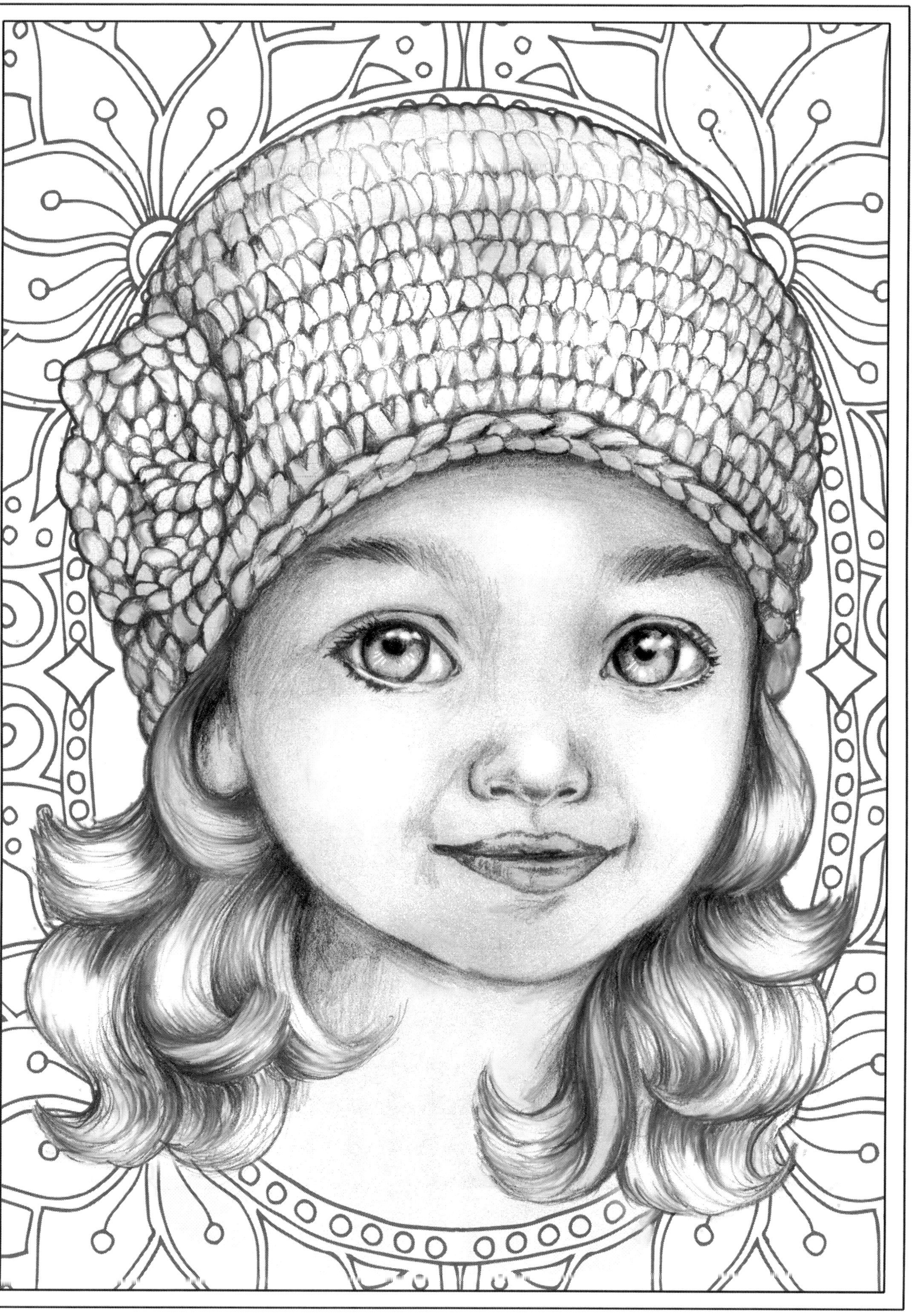

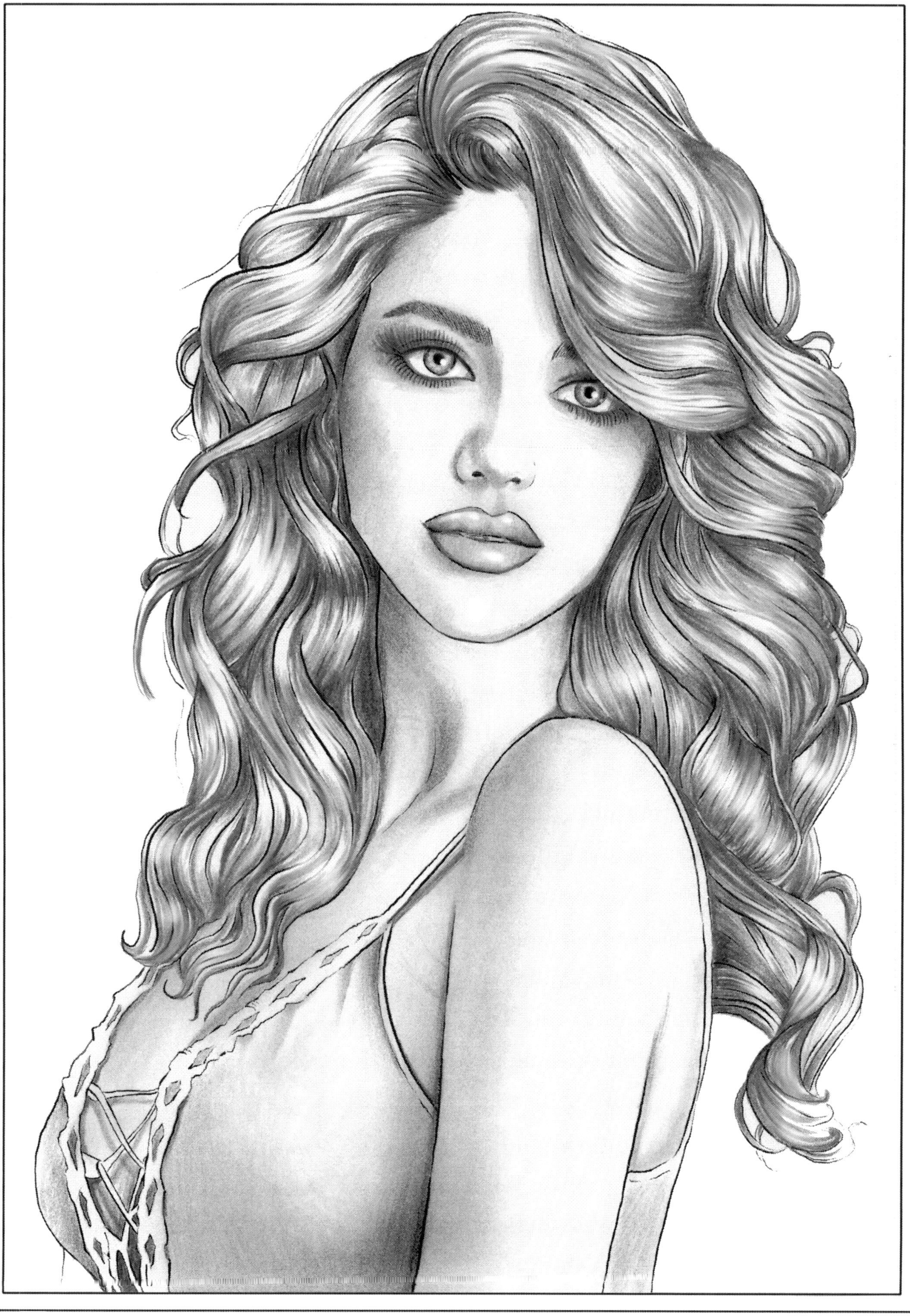

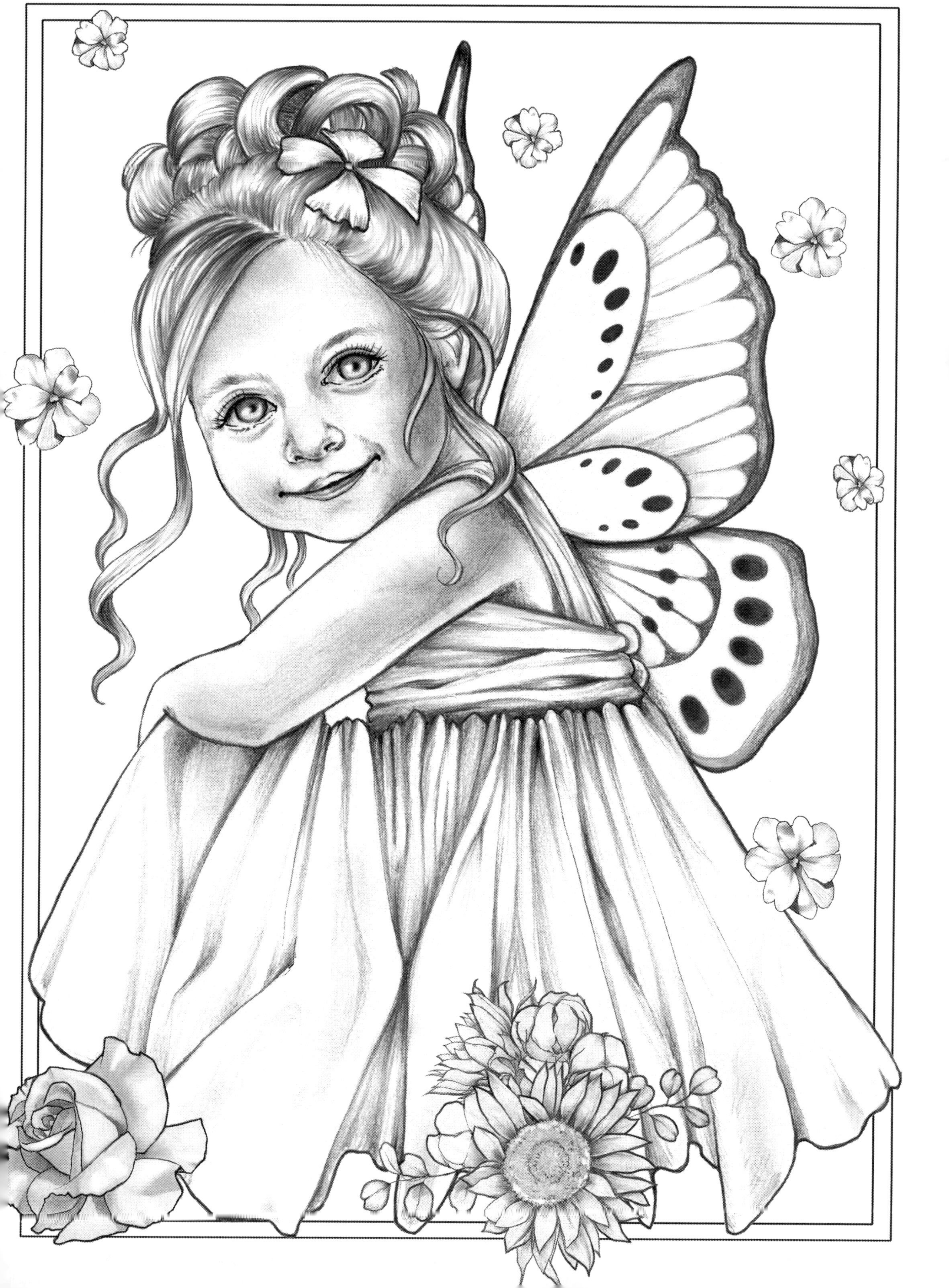

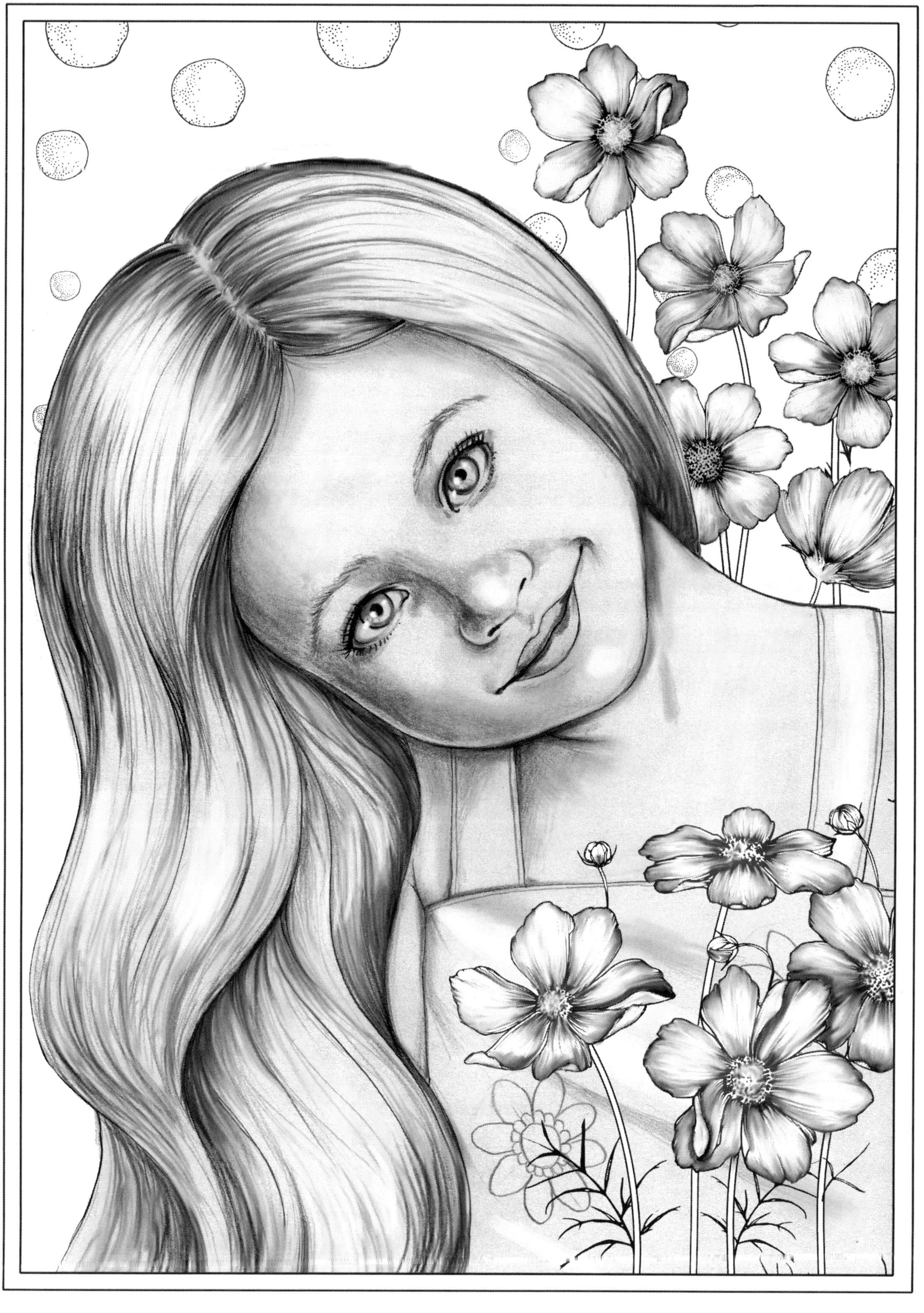

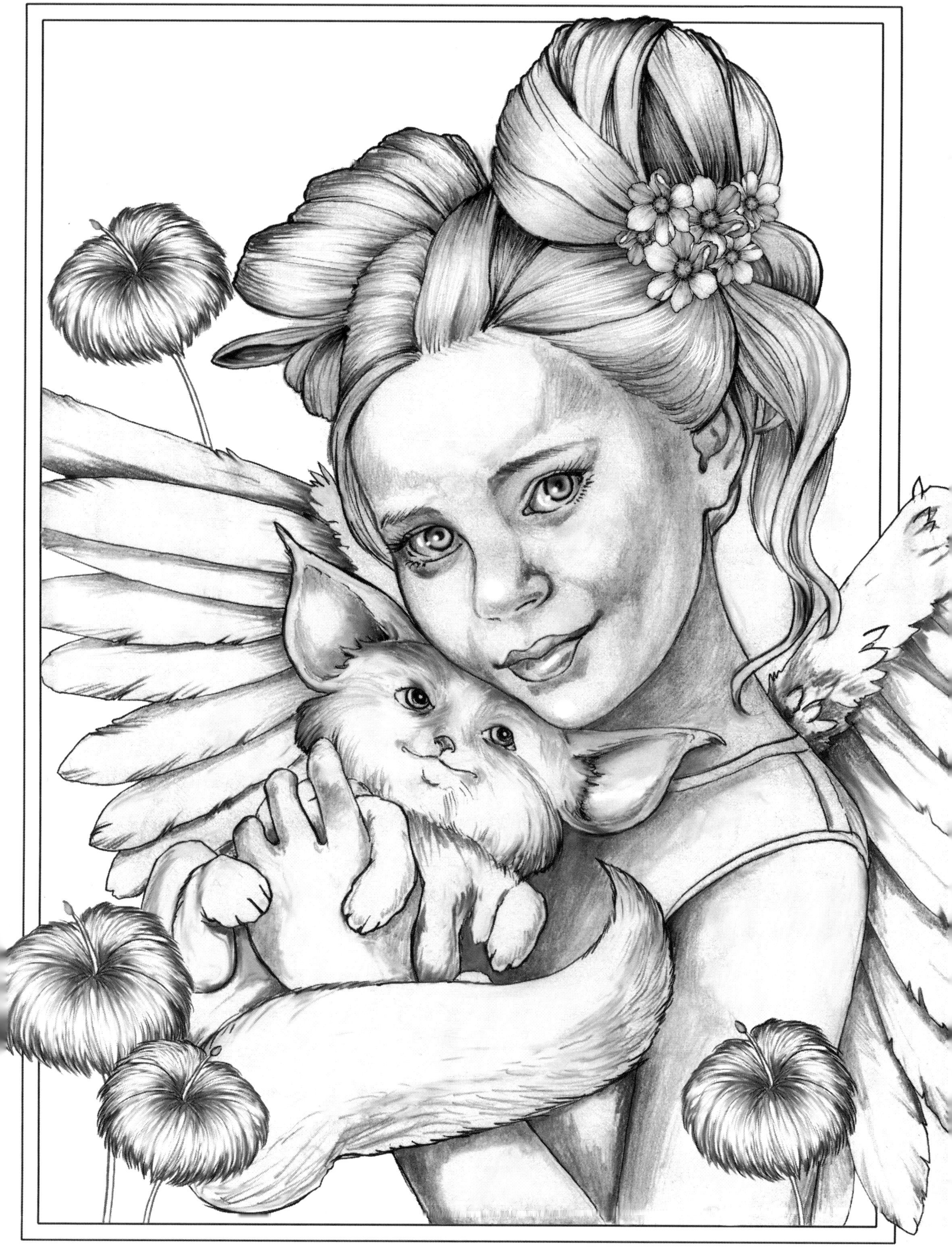

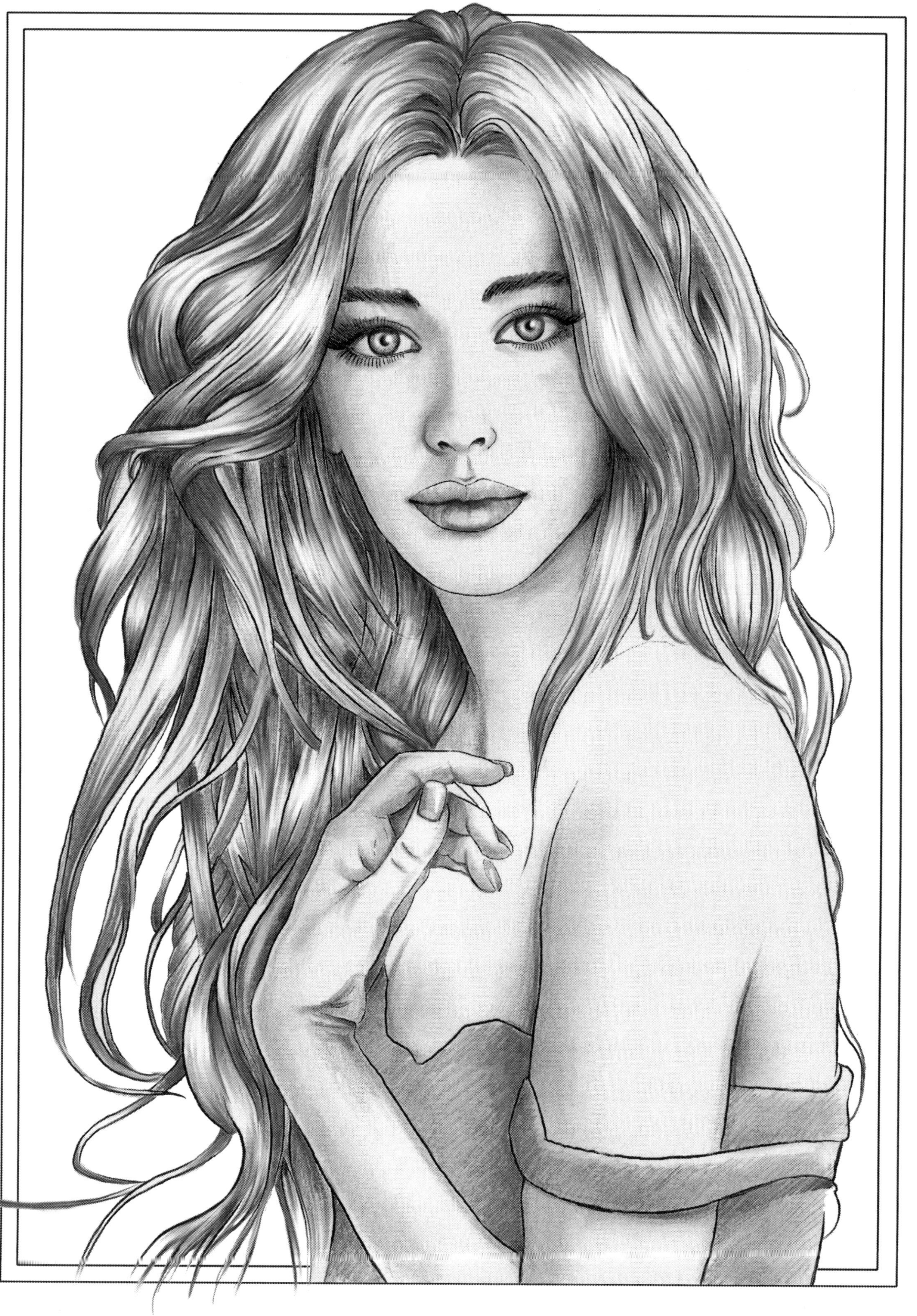

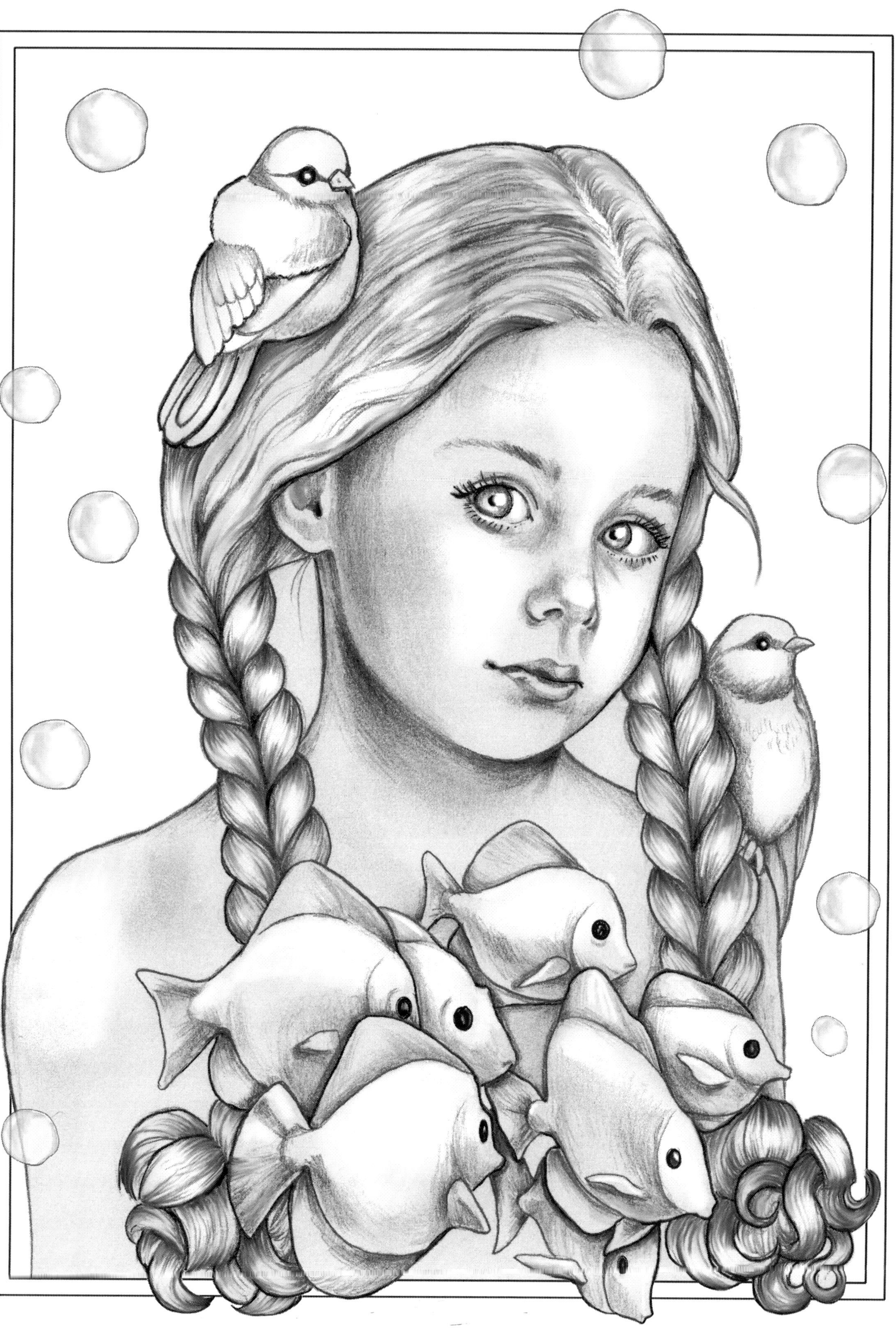

Made in the USA
Las Vegas, NV
22 November 2022

59940500R00046